In the beginning
Sky spanned the heavens
and Earth lay firm below.

And in its time
and in its way
came a union of the Two:
Father Sky and Mother Earth.

And Father Sky sent down two rays of sun to warm his bride.

And then, lest she become dry and parched,
he followed with a gentle rain.
To moisten.
To germinate.
To nurture.

And through this union the loom took form.

As its top—the boundless sky.
As its base—the massive earth.
Beaming sunrays the uprights
and streaming rain—the warp.

Then spanning the top to keep warp tight:
A lightning bolt, so it is said.

Then in the crowning moments
a Shell-White comb appeared
sacred in its hue and substance
essential in its use and purpose.
One final touch to go:

For this,
Halo Of The Sun
came down.

He beamed down his potency.
He shaped a batten strong and straight.
He penetrated through the sheds
and spread the warp to give it air
and spread the warp to let it breathe.

And thus he gave it life.

HALO OF THE SUN

Stories Told and Retold

BY NOËL BENNETT
PHOTOGRAPHS BY JOHN RUNNING

 Northland Press / Flagstaff, Arizona

To Brock and Jim
and Starry Tent-Rock Nights

Cover photograph, John Running
Text copyright 1987 by Shared Horizons
Photographs copyright 1987 by John Running
ALL RIGHTS RESERVED
First Edition
ISBN 0-87358-437-6 softcover
Library of Congress Catalog Card Number 86-46366
Printed and Bound in the United States of America
Design by David Jenney

This project was sponsored by
Shared Horizons through grants from the
L. J. Skaggs and Mary C. Skaggs Foundation
and the Weatherhead Foundation.

Preface

I am an Anglo woman nearing fifty. At the age of twenty-eight, in 1968, I went to the Navajo Reservation with my physician-husband and son. We intended to stay two years.

I had been born into a cross-cultural family. Studied art in college. Was an exchange student in Europe. Had even taken up Anglo weaving before coming. But I was really unprepared for being with the Navajo.

We stayed eight years.

I stayed because there were lessons to learn. While I was carding, spinning and weaving, I was learning. I was learning what it is that must be passed from Grandmother to Mother to Daughter. The importance of interacting with the elements. The power of the oral tradition. The essentiality of ritual. And silence. The sacredness of being gifted a story.

The Navajo have a saying that after two years they'll decide if they'll be your friend. They also use the word "stingy" for how they are with their knowledge and stories. Time is nothing. But a story is a source of power.

I will tell you something about stories.
They aren't just entertainment.
Don't be fooled.
They are all we have, you see,
all we have to fight off
illness and death.

You don't have anything
if you don't have stories.

He rubbed his belly.
I keep them here.
Here, put your hand on it.
See, it is moving.
There is life here
for the people.*

Telling a story is a sacred act. And the storyteller and listener must both be ripe.

The teller holds the story. Then, word by word by nuance recreates it. Speeds up to cover terrain, slows down to carve a channel. In perfect time, reveals the whole.

The listener sheds anything that blocks the flow. Doesn't judge while being told. Hears the words. A part of the void—the empty vessel, receiving.

*Ceremony by Leslie Marmon Silko

Stories are owned. And kept. And told. Each telling is a risk. A test of the teller's strength. The right words must be eked out. Saying aloud brings into Beingness.

Now twenty years later, I no longer live on reservation. But the Navajo stories and the stories that came from my being there still have relevance. And I still tell them.

In making this book, I had to find a way to write what I am used to giving with my voice. And many people helped.

The book began with the courage and vision of Tiana Bighorse, Helen Tsinnie, and the other Navajo weavers who entrusted me their weaving stories.

A Weatherhead Foundation grant in 1975 enabled me to write the legends and John Running to make the photographs. An L. J. Skaggs and Mary C. Skaggs Foundation grant in 1986 enabled the completion of the project through Shared Horizons.

The stories are indebted to Patricia Clark Smith, who helped to carve them out. Timothy M. Sheehan volunteered legal assistance at my every turn. Irvy Goosen lent accuracy to our rendering of the Navajo language. And John Running's friendship and belief in the project has spanned the full twenty years of this book's making.

Perhaps the reader will collaborate:

Read the stories aloud.
And give them life.

In olden days
White-Shell-Woman lived.
She wore perfect white.
She walked with perfect grace.
She was a perfect vessel:
Essential Womanliness.

One morning wandering in the white of dawn
she came upon a stream of smoke
wafting skyward from the ground.
With wonder she approached the Earth-hole.
Innocently peered within.

There in the dusky depths,
there in musty dimness,
an Old-One worked
tying a thread
weaving a web.

This was the home of Spiderwoman.

Down in her earth-lined chamber, Spiderwoman wove.
A shadow blocked her light above.
An astonished face looked in.

"Come down into my home,"
Spiderwoman directed.

"It is too small,"
White-Shell-Woman objected.

"It is big enough,"
Dark Black Weaver insisted.

And so saying
Began to blow.

HALO OF THE SUN   XV

At the hole she blew—
at the entrance overhead.
Again and again she blew,
Four times in all It is said.

With each puff the portal opened
widened, grew and swelled,
until a passageway stood large enough
and four ladders lined the walls.

On the East was a White ladder
with rungs of shell—
the color of dawn.
On the South was a Blue ladder
with rungs of turquoise—
the color of sky at noon.
On the West was a Red ladder
with rungs of abalone—
the color of the setting sun.
On the North the ladder was Black.
Its rungs were jet.

For that is the color of night.

Gusts Picked At The Edges Of The Silted Earth, first gently, then with growing vigor, until a mauve haze obscured the flat sageland before me. I urged my son to hurry. In his small hand he clenched a worn food card. On the back a young Navajo man two days before had drawn an intricate map to his mother's hogan. His mother, a weaver.

Shawn, six, was my moral support, a help in countering my failing resolve. I had been on reservation less than a week. There were at least two years ahead during which to leisurely find a weaver. Learning Navajo weaving couldn't require two years of motivated, concerted effort. I could go next week. . . .

I headed the car down the road.

Finding a weaver had not been easy. The terse traders, Navajo rugs piled about them, knew of none. The urbane doctor's wives, unventuring in their year of stay, knew of none. My husband Jack, home from his first day at the new hospital, had encountered none.

As we turned onto the rutted road at the trading post, the cards to comb the wool bounced beside me and I steadied them. Already they were looking used.

Two days before, Jack, home for lunch amidst packing boxes, had listened sympathetically to my frustration in finding a weaver. When he left for the hospital, I lay down for a nap, but no sooner had I closed my eyes when I heard him open the door again.

"I know you need a rest. But I know you'll like it even less if I go to work without telling you. There's a lady sitting in the brush herding sheep—and she's combing her wool!"

I hurried across sand and sage toward a distant figure bleached in noon-day glare. With mild curiousity she watched me. At close range her dark, bright eyes and rutted skin caused me to hesitate. I didn't speak Navajo; she probably didn't speak English. I settled beside her in the sun.

"Hello."

She spoke in Navajo and continued carding: wool on the left card, just the right amount; right card on top; a series of long combing motions; a quick double sliding push-pull.

She was carding with her back to her flock. Behind her I could see sheep grazing contentedly in prime Tuba City pasturage—Anglo doctors' lawns. Approximately every half-hour she glanced about. "Surprised" at seeing the sheep nibbling in gardens, she jumped up and herded them back to the barren sagebrush and then resumed carding. While I watched, the sheep made their way back to greener grass. After two hours, she suddenly got up, flung a word melodically into the silence, and left. Her sheep with her.

Within minutes I was on my way to the trading post to buy my own cards. Back home I positioned wool and cards precisely as I had seen her do. Comb. Grate. Mesh. She had turned her wool to silk, mine was now matted. I continued to practice. At the end of the day, sitting by a pile of jumbled wool rolls, I resolved to find a weaver to teach me.

Years before, as a foreign exchange student in Germany, I had sat on cobblestones and painted village scenes. Soon the local children discovered the "artista." Not long afterwards parents came to get their kids—and peek at the painting. A conversation was initiated.

Then a lunch invitation. Suddenly, there we were eating brautwurst and black bread.

So maybe if I sat in the middle of town carding, someone would help me learn. All I needed was a good location and enough courage. Tuba City options were limited: two trading posts, an elementary school, a Dairy Queen, one gas station and the laundromat.

The women do the laundry and the women do the weaving. I piled dirty clothes into the jeep, cards and wool on top. Half an hour later, laundry turning inside machines, I sat on the ground outside and began to card. Women and children took notice and stood near, forming a circle. No one said a word. Time went by. I began to realize Tuba City wasn't Beutelsbach.

No one pitied my clumsiness with the cards. No matter how much difficulty I encountered, no one offered help. No advice. No words at all. Just a soft easy giggle occasionally rippling around the growing circle. There was nothing to do but continue. Intently. Completely. With singleness of mind.

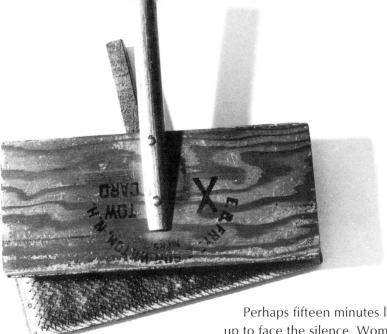

Perhaps fifteen minutes later I looked up to face the silence. Women were now three deep about me. A black pick-up was pulling to a stop at the edge of the crowd, a young man and woman were getting out. Slowly the woman came over and knelt beside me.

"What are you doing?"
It wasn't a positive, inquisitive—"What are you doing?" Nor was it a negative, derogatory—"What are you doing!" The inflection was neutral. Flat. Balanced just in between.

"I'm trying to card wool."
Dead silence.
Wrong answer! Could have said anything but that.

An inner dialogue filled in the unnerving space. I desparately wished someone would help me, so I said aloud,

"I'm having a hard time."
Silence.
Self-evident. Words wasted on the obvious. Don't talk now till she does.

I began a new batch of wool, intent on matching her reserve. I came to the end. Still she hadn't spoken. I laid another wool roll on the pile.

"Can you help me?"
Silence.
"Just keep carding."
I know, now, her answer was the best that could have been given—my mind knew the method; my hands had yet to refine pressure and rhythm. But that was not what I wanted to hear. I wanted real help: "You're holding the cards wrong. You're using too much pressure. Too much wool."

But the silence had been broken. And questions now bobbed up in various parts of the circle, then traveled in Navajo around the perimeter. When they came to the young woman, she translated.

"They want to know where you get your wool."

"It's my mother's sheep," I answered, knowing that with the Navajo, sheep belong to the women. "From California." Translation into Navajo. Hands reaching to feel "California wool." Again, indistinguishable clicks and stops coming the course of the circle.

"What color is it?" Lips pointed toward the dirty wool before me. The question was odd to me. I answered the obvious.

"It's white." Then clarified, "I haven't washed it yet." The translation went around but quickly came back.

"They think it's grey; they can't believe it's white."

I looked at my dirty white wool. Mixed with black California soil, it was grey. Maybe the Navajo white wool, mixed with red Arizona soil, would be pink. I shared the thought. Many hands reached in the bag and my mother's sheep disappeared into the circle.

The next question came quickly. "They want to know who's training you."

The wording was strange to me, but the question was in the right place. I took my time with the answer. There was a beauty in not having to blurt out the first thing that came to mind. "Nobody. . . Yesterday I watched an old lady carding in the sagebrush. . . . I'd like to learn more."

Stillness. Stillness. Unrelenting stillness.

"Do you know anyone who could teach me?"

As soon as I heard my own words, I chided myself. I had now asked twice. I returned to carding. In the time it took to process three more wool rolls, the woman from the pick-up began to speak.

"My mother-in-law weaves." My heart pounded hopefully. "She's a good weaver." Another wool-roll later. "She sells her rugs at the Cameron Trading Post."

"Would she teach me?".

"You ask her. She speaks good English."

Her husband drew the map on the back of a food card. The woman, Clara, assured me I could come any time. I loaded the now very clean, wet clothes, the worn food card, and what was left of Mom's wool in the back of the jeep. I drove off with one of the first headaches of my life.

Here we were now—past the trading post, past the fork, taking the road behind the mountain, past the turn to the right we were not supposed to take and now we were heading down the road to her hogan.

The night before I had attended a lecture on patient etiquette given by a Navajo man to new doctors at the hospital. Afterward, I told him I would be visiting a weaver the next morning. Was there anything I should know?

Don't park right in front of the hogan door. The hogan is one room. If you stop right in front and the door is open, you can see inside the hogan and you will know if somebody's in there. If they're there and don't want to come out, they just stay inside. So it's better you don't know if they're there. That way everybody saves face. And don't get right out. Just wait awhile. Someone will come out if they want to see you; not if they don't.

So Shawn and I waited together. Children emerged, circling the car, peering in windows. I was uncertain how they counted in the etiquette; if children acknowledged our presence, was it all

right to get out? Or did we need to wait for an adult to welcome us? After five minutes, we got out and slowly walked across the camp toward the black pick-up we had first seen at the laundry.

"What do you want?"

A handsome young man had come out of the hogan. Perfect English; unreadable expression. Not a cordial "Can-I-help-you-What-do-you-want?" Nor a hostile "What-are-you-doing-here-What-do-you-want?" Just between. I asked for Clara. He looked away, then gestured toward the hogan. "She's brushing her hair."

Clara paused in the hogan doorway, brush in hand, shiny black hair hanging long and free. She eyed me uncertainly as though wondering why I had come.

"I just came to see about weaving." Her expression didn't change. "Did you ask your mother-in-law?"

She went back to brushing her hair. I felt the ticking of seconds and then minutes. Then she stopped.

"Yes."

Silence.

"What did she say?" I felt a growing

impatience as I rephrased the obvious. These silences were grating on me, underscoring my position as an outsider. I considered leaving.

"She hasn't answered yet."

I almost laughed aloud at her reply. I felt the tension leave. They weren't treating me, the Anglo, differently. Long silence was the Navajo way.

I began to look about me, in no hurry now to talk. There was time to savor colors and textures. The children's bare feet and the red dark earth blended as one; a pile of untanned sheep skins lay over a smooth rail fence. Adults had joined the circle, their faces neither friendly nor unfriendly.

"You ask her. She speaks good English."

I looked at Clara and saw her gesture toward a woman standing in shadow to my left. Clothed in long traditional satin skirt and velvet blouse, she looked about fifty and yet seemed ageless. Her feet were solidly together, arms folded before her. How long had she been there? Could it be she did speak English? *If* she understood English, *if* Clara had asked her, or even if she had heard Clara and me talking, she would know why I had come. I had, in effect, already asked. So I simply smiled.

There was no response. But then her expression began to change. She shifted her weight, and slowly crossed the packed earth to the sheep corral. In one clean motion she pulled a goat skin off the rail. Tufted white was swept aside to reveal shimmering golds and rusts. A rug in progress. And color enough to fill all sound and space.

I stepped forward. My fingertips scanned the surface: soft, earthy lanolin; rhythmic joints possible only through years of repetition.

"It's beautiful. Clara said you were a good weaver and you are." Words blurted forth against the silence I meant to keep. I couldn't help it. It was a statement of truth, the kind that needs no answer.

One came anyway—a clear voice seeking seldom-used words.

"I should be. I've been weaving since I was seven."

That was my meeting with Tiana Bighorse. Later, when I did formally ask if she would teach me, her reply was equally to the point.

"How long do you have to learn?"

I would be in Tuba City two years. There seemed no better answer. But I waited for what I thought to be an appropriate time then confidently said:

"Two years." Her expression clouded and I hastily added, "Will that be enough?"

She shifted her eyes. Downward, then back at me.

"Perhaps."

It has been twenty years since that meeting day. Many times I have recalled the economical words of a woman who had been weaving almost half a century spoken to a young stranger wanting to undertake the craft. And with the passing of time I have come to further understand. Two years was not nearly enough.

Descending
into the damp dimness
White-Shell-Woman looked around her.
Woven forms surrounded her.
Beautiful to behold!

"Yes, I made them all.
That's what I do.
And WHAT do YOU do?"
Inquired the Dark Black Weaver.

White-Shell-Woman considered
the question with care:

She thought about the way she had lived
for so long.
She thought about the corn she had ground
for so long.
She thought about the empty void
she had felt for so long.

"It's not good doing nothing,"
White-Shell-Woman concluded
sitting down wistfully.

"It's not good doing nothing,"
Spiderwoman repeated
and retreated to her web.

White-Shell-Woman watched
the quiet twining
fingers working
designs unfolding.
Something for the hand to do
for the eye to see
for the mind to hold.

"Maybe, if I watch you weave,
twine the color, shape the web,
maybe then I can learn your Way."

From the Spider.
No response.
Just continued weaving.
But Shell-Woman,
watching the Ancient One work,
started to feel hopeful.

Henry Clark Was A Navajo Silversmith.

He had taught at Navajo Community College and spoke English. I thought his work classically elegant and often brought him turquoise to set.

One day as I handed him a small bag of stones, I asked him about how long it would be until he could make them into rings. I carefully phrased my question to reflect the open, unstructured time sense of the reservation which has little to do with clocks and calendars; "Anglo Time"—precise appointments and advanced planning—was a familiar joke among the Navajo. Henry replied he could have them done by the following Wednesday, thereby surprising me by his preciseness. Was he phrasing his reply in Anglo Time for my benefit? Was this a remnant of his college teaching? Further, he told me he'd be in Gallup, could bring the rings by my house and save me a trip. This was the first time he had offered to come to my house. I gave him clear directions.

When Wednesday came and he didn't, I assumed Henry really was on Navajo time after all. Nor did I worry on Thursday. Maybe a ceremony had come up, or maybe he had to drive his family to Utah. Perhaps his son had shot a deer and Henry had to butcher it and tan the skin. Friday I figured he would show up over the weekend. By Monday I was getting tired of staying home in case I'd miss him, but I thought I'd better give him until next Wednesday before going out to see what had happened.

Wednesday morning I drove to his house and waited in the jeep according to protocol. He appeared immediately, bringing the jewelry with him.

"Where were you last Wednesday?" It was *Henry* who asked the question.

"Home."

"I came to your house with the turquoise."

"I was home all day, how could I have missed you?"

Oh, no. Could he have sat in the driveway in the pickup and waited for me to come out? I never look out the window to see if anyone is there. The door of my Anglo home doesn't even face the driveway.

I suggested that next time he should just come to the door and knock.

"I can't come to the door of your house!" He sounded taken aback.

"Well, why not?"

"Because the neighbors are going to think I'm about to steal something."

"That's not true, Henry. Lots of Navajo friends visit me all the time. If you come to the door, it'll be okay."

He didn't say anything—just gave me the jewelry. I handed him another package of stones for rings. "When do you think they'll be done?"

"Next Wednesday."

Wednesday I stayed home again. Every once in a while I looked outside, just to be sure he wasn't there. Then toward the end of the day I heard the knock. With a warm feeling, I opened the door. Nobody was there.

Then I spotted him. He was waiting in his pickup.

One Doctor Spent All His Off-Time With Seed Catalogs,

seeking superior stock. He wanted to bring the same kind of scientific professionalism to his vegetable garden in Tuba City as he did to his practice. The soil had never been worked before and might have to be balanced with lime, iron, and bonemeal. So he wrote the U.S.D.A. to ask how to obtain a complete soil analysis. He received an immediate answer that the service was free. He need only send a sample.

I, too, had a garden. And each time I saw him I asked whether he had received the test results. The answer was continually "No." Three months passed. At first, we agitated about the delay. Eventually chalked it off to government bureaucracy. Growing season gave way to fall, fall to winter and agitation to disgust.

"Probably some fool government worker lost my soil under all his paper!"

But just before planting time the following spring, a small brown package came into the Tuba City Hospital mail room, addressed from the U.S.D.A. A neatly scribed letter was enclosed.

Dear Doctor,

Please accept my apologies for the delay in your soil sample analysis. As I could tell from the tone of your letter that the results were very important to you, I took the necessary time to be clear in my diagnosis. Enclosed please find my best advice regarding your soil. Good Luck.

Inside was a carefully wrapped, small, hand-made clay pot.

From Master-Weaver,
from Seer-Beyond-The-Time.
Four days Shell-Woman stayed
and received the knowledge of weaving.

Each morning the two approached the loom:
one to weave
one to watch.
And what they began each dawn
by noon was to the half.

Then Old-Weaver
climbed her hole
and there she spun a web.
She threw it high
and looped the sun
and pulled it overhead.
Then back below and back to work
the loom resumed again.
And so continued in this way
till web and day
were done.

Four days.
Four rugs.
Each a different color.
Each a different design.
For each of four directions.

Time came for the two to part,
for each to bid their bye.

"I go my way
fulfilled, at one,"
White-Shell-Woman began.

"That is good,"
Old-Spinner spoke,
"But there is one thought more:
Remember me
and these four days.
Remember the Spider
who showed you the way.
And whenever you weave
just think of me—
and leave a hole
and weave a hole
as I do in my web." *

---

*In the old days, weavers concealed a small hole in
each rug they wove in tribute to Spiderwoman.

Irvy Goosen Raised His Hand To Indicate Changing Pitch.

"Since Navajo is a tonal language, we'll be singing it. I will be conductor; repeat after me.

"Yá'át'ééh." (Hello)

"Yá'át'ééh," the class chorused.

"Yá'át'ééh, Shimá." (Hello, my mother)

"Yá'át'ééh, Shimá," we repeated.

"Yá'át'ééh, Shimá dóó Shizhé'é." (Hello, my mother and my father)

As the phrases lengthened and complicated, I dropped behind, unable to repeat these sequential nonsense syllables. I contented myself with listening to those who could.

This was the first night of my Navajo language class. I was no linguist and was going to have to study hard to learn this especially difficult language. Our professor's text sat before me on the desk. Its title, *Navajo Made Easier*, underscored the challenge.

I scanned the room, listening to the foreign sounds I would have to learn to make. Most students were as lost as I. One soft-spoken Navajo man, who was in the class to learn to write his own

language, was an exception. The other was a vocal Anglo behind me. Obviously relishing the complexity of the sounds, he was confidently booming back Irvy's lengthening sentences. After class, I introduced myself and asked where he got his obvious ease with the sounds.

"Well, you see, I'm a linguistics major," Bill said. "I've studied Russian; it was easy. Mandarin Chinese was more difficult, but beautiful. I can't wait for Navajo."

That week at home I practiced Lesson One dutifully. I played the tape that accompanied the book, and repeated the sounds until they flowed as smoothly as my well-practiced carding motions. The second class, all through Irvy's review of Lesson One, I sang the phrases back. However, as soon as he launched into unstudied territory, I again fell silent. Bill kept right on booming it back.

I was well prepared again the following week and got so caught up in class I hardly noticed that Bill was now talking it back. The fourth session, Bill was silent. The fifth, he didn't come. He never showed up again.

Some months later, I saw Bill at the trading post and asked why he'd dropped. His explanation was to the point: "Russian is easy. Mandarin Chinese is difficult but beautiful. . . . But you can have your Navajo!"

The Navajo language was successfully used to transmit messages in the Pacific during World War II. Through Navajo code talkers, secrets were radioed behind the lines. The Japanese—thinking it to be a code—were completely unable to decipher it.

Part of the complexity of the language is the verbs. The different voices—first, second, third person, plus a polite third person—are highly irregular. In addition to action, verbs must indicate singular, dual, plural or distributive depending on the number of actors or recipients of action. They must contain both subject and object. So each makes a complete sentence.

In English we use the verb phrase, "pick-it-up," to refer to any object. However, in Navajo, verbs relating to the positioning or handling of items entail twelve classes. And a roundish or bulky object; a long, slender object; a flexible, thin object; something in a container— each has its own verb stem.

Tonality (changing pitch) can alter the meaning of otherwise identical sounds. Clicks, nasals, glottal stops, aspirations— most have no equivalent in English.

To help us master these sounds, Irvy had us memorize a tongue-twister phrase containing all the sounds in the Navajo language. Though Shawn and I knew it was a bit silly, and certainly unusable, we practiced it continually around the house—even showed it off to Anglo visitors at every opportunity. "Sik'is bitł'ízí t'óó ahayóí ńt'éé' ndi k'ad ádin." Translation: My friend used to have lots of goats but doesn't have any anymore.

After months of practicing from the book and tape, I had useful phrases I could say, but it was almost impossible to understand what someone was saying to me. To gain more skill, I would pick up

Navajo hitchhikers whenever I was out driving, especially the older, more traditional people who spoke no English.

One day I stopped to give an old lady a lift. As she got into the car I began my limited phrases:

"Hello, my Grandmother." I said as clearly as possible from Lesson One.

"Hello, my Granddaughter," she replied. So far so good.

"Where are you going, my Grandmother?" I recited from Lesson Two.

A flood of Navajo words returned, not one of which was understandable—only gestures that told me to keep going straight ahead and eventually we would turn.

Starting out in the indicated direction, I searched for a better topic.

"How many children do you have, my Grandmother?"

Her answer contained the number eleven. Then after the Navajo word for grandchildren, a much higher number I had not yet memorized, and some small numbers—maybe those who had predeceased her. She gestured for me to turn onto the dirt road ahead.

Steering the car along the bumpy road and the conversation to a more familiar vocabulary, I asked "Are you a weaver, my Grandmother?"

I listened hopefully for the word "Yes." If she wove, I could draw on my weaving vocabulary: dah 'iistł'ǫ́, loom; 'aghaa', wool; bee 'adizí, spindle; and the names of various dye plants growing by the side of the road. Instead, I heard another flood of Navajo words: "Shiłʼízí t'óó ahayóí ńt'éé ndi k'ad ádin." I grinned. She hadn't said "Yes," but I had understood every word she had said:

"I used to have a lot of goats, but I don't have any anymore!"

One morning at dawn
in her hogan alone
White-Shell-Woman began to weave.

In Spiderwoman's way
she built a loom
and stretched a web.
Slowly.
Precisely.
With care.

Four days
four nights
she applied herself.
But everything went wrong.
Though she tried with patience
though she twined with aptness,
yet the web would break.

First frustration then mistrust:
"Can beauty really come of this?"

Then faint and disheartened
she raveled the web
disheveled the loom
cast out the tangled mess
and left.
To rest.

The Legendary Spiderwoman Insisted White Shell Woman Learn To Spin Before Learning To Weave.

Tiana Bighorse advised me similarly. However, as it turned out, I so loved spinning and dyeing that six months later I was still caught in its web. I walked all elevations of the reservation, seeking native plants and learning to evoke their muted hues. A hundred and twenty colored skeins later my weaving mentor, in a tone suggesting the honeymoon was over, asked when I was going to learn to weave.

So I made a loom of cedar and began my first weaving. If I had continued following tradition, the rug would have been striped. But, having not been long on reservation, my Anglo eagerness set the design and I began instead a sampler rug—one to combine all my dyed yarns with as many techniques as possible. It was to become a sampler of challenges.

I was just beginning my first design in colors from wild carrot and cedar bark, when son Shawn came to sit on my lap mid-row. Wanting to bring him into the experience, I asked him what design

should follow. "A snake, a stick and the sun," he said.

The serpent from San Ildefonso offered itself as a prototype for the snake. Another Navajo friend, Helen Tsinnie,— "Philosophic Weaver"—helped me begin. We used an especially difficult technique including repetitive triangles for tail and tongue spears, ornate horning for the head. Weaving it in, unraveling, weaving it right . . . through time and persistence the snake came into being.

The stick and tufted sun were next followed by a design in two-face, where both sides of the weaving are different. Again the complexity was absorbing and I felt proud and relieved getting through this really difficult part. Vowing never again to weave another two-face, I unknowingly began my greatest test.

It started quietly one morning when a Navajo family came to visit. Grandmother. Mother. Daughter. Like most Navajo visitors, they walked about the house, looking at everything, interested in how the Anglo family lived. I understood, for I enjoyed being in Navajo hogans. I took

my visitors for a tour of the livingroom, showing them the Navajo loom with its growing sampler, proud of the two-face band I had just completed. Next I demonstrated the Anglo treadle loom on the far side of the room. Like these visitors, Navajo weavers were always fascinated by the heddles and pedals. But, sometime during the demonstration, I noticed Grandmother had not moved from the Navajo loom and was now speaking loudly in Navajo. Her gestures were agitated. I asked Mother what Grandmother was saying.

"It is nothing," she shrugged.

I continued on, showing the three women my many skeins of dyed yarns. I used the Navajo names of specific dye-plants, hoping Grandmother would be able to understand and perhaps feel more included. Grandmother didn't move. She was still by the loom, talking. Clearly she was upset. This time I turned to Granddaughter. What was bothering Grandmother? Again a laughing, off-hand remark—something old-fashioned Grandmother was rattling on about. Speaking quietly again to Mother, I told

her I cared very much about old-time beliefs. I would like to hear what Grandmother wanted me to know. With this gentle urging the Mother began.

Grandmother was talking about a worry, an old-time belief. It was bad luck to weave a snake in a rug. Violating the taboo could bring harmful consequences. I was taken aback. What could I do to right my mistake. Take the rug off the loom and not finish it?

"No. The rug would still be there."

"Take it off and burn it?" I offered. I thought about hours of painstaking work, and my attachment to each of the difficult designs.

"No, it would still exist."

The only solution, Grandmother said, was to unravel the whole piece, row by row.

After my guests had left, I sat gazing at my weaving. I could not bring myself to begin the unraveling. So much of myself had been woven into it; taking it out would be a personal loss. I stopped weaving.

Unaware of what had happened since her last visit, Helen Tsinnie stopped by.

She said I had made good progress. During a quiet moment, I told her about Grandmother's visit. I asked if she had ever heard of such a taboo. Yes, she admitted after a pause. Her mother had done it once—woven a big, black snake from bottom to top. Everyone who had seen it had told her not to do it. They said it would bring danger. They told her it would make her blind. But she did it anyway.

The night she was finishing her rug, it was stormy. Thunder and lightning came close together, again and again. As she untied the rug from the loom, the night loosed its anger. Lightning struck and killed two horses: one she used to herd the sheep, one she used to tighten the loom. It was only then she understood: Snake and Lightning are one. They work together for harm.

"How come I wasn't told of this taboo before starting the snake?"

My friend thought for a long time, then said, "It isn't bad luck if you don't believe in it."

Helen had thought it would be all right for an Anglo to weave a snake. She had

not foreseen I would take in Navajo weaving in such depth—technique *and* belief.

There was a further pause, then, "I think I made a mistake. If something happens to you—maybe not till next week, or next month or next year—if something happens to you they'll say it's because you put a snake in the rug. And," she added, "if nothing happens, they'll say it's because you're a witch."

I put away my weaving tools.

Six months later I was in a trading post, looking at pawn jewelry about to be sold. While I was admiring the pieces, a Navajo lady came up behind me and pointed to three specific items: "That's mine, that's mine, and that's mine." Turning, I recognized Tiana Bighorse. As she had no money to redeem her pieces, I offered what little I had to buy one back for her. Which did she like best? A Zuni inlaid bracelet that her daughter had given her for Mothers Day. I examined it closely. The design was of a beautiful big eagle, with wings outstretched. And between beak and both talons stretched a snake.

"Isn't it bad luck to have a snake in a

bracelet?" I asked quietly.

She looked at me pointedly. "Why should it be bad luck?"

I moved on to the cashier, also a friend. While paying, I again asked the question.

"Of course not." She eyed me curiously. I began to think I had the strange beliefs.

Then on the way to the car, as Tiana Bighorse was putting the bracelet back on her wrist, she paused.

"You buy this back for me so I tell you. It *is* bad luck to put a snake in a bracelet. My son try to get it off. He don't have the right tools." She pointed to hack marks outside the beak and beside both talons. "But it's O.K. The Snake is about to be food for the Eagle."

There it was! When I got home later that afternoon, I excitedly ran inside yelling to my family, "What bird eats more snakes than any other?"

"Roadrunner," Shawn and Jack yelled back simultaneously from different parts of the house.

Right then I sat down and wove two roadrunners into the top of my rug.

From that day on, if any traditional Navajo weavers even started to look at the serpent, I'd say quickly, "Hey, it's O.K. If that snake makes a move, those roadrunners will be down to get him in a moment."

Years later, I gave a lecture at the Denver Museum of Natural History and told this story of my first weaving. Bertha Stevens, Navajo weaver, was in the audience. Through the years, she and her medicineman-sandpainter husband, Fred Stevens, had traveled and demonstrated extensively throughout the world.

Bertha is of the culture that holds the snake taboo. But she has broken with Navajo tradition by excelling openly as an individual. When the lecture was over, Bertha waited until the entire crowd had left. Then she came to talk with me. She had listened with understanding to my story and wanted to give me something.

"I want you to remember," she told me.

"You have always walked in Beauty. All you have to do is keep going."

With the first faint
traces of the dawn
White-Shell-Woman arose.
Singing seemed to call to her
from within her home.
Slowly she approached the dwelling,
arriving as the chanting ended,
and a voice from out of nowhere
bid White-Shell-Woman
"Come-in."

Stepping slowly though the doorway
she sat down quietly
looked about her.

In awesome splendor,
she saw them there.
In flowing beauty,
she saw them there.
Bedecked in buckskin
they were there.
Laden with turquoise
they were there.
They were the Holy Ones.

She saw them standing,
knew their being,
then her glance swept on beyond.
Rising up behind the conclave
haloed in the morning sunlight
her loom against the hogan siding
stood perfectly restored.

Not till then did she know the purpose.
Not till then did the holy ones speak.
Their chosen words were slow in coming.
She listened fully.
Received their meaning.

"The loom, my child,
is life itself.
The weaving-way holds beauty.

The loom, my child
is breath itself.
The weaving-way holds power.

Through weaving one can come to know
the meaning of life and breath.

Through weaving one can come to be
strong and self-sufficient.

Return to your loom.
Resume your work.
Spin your web of *wool*.
And as you weave
and as you work,
Life's Truths will come to you."

There Is No Navajo Word For "Thank You."

"Ahéhee'," the closest, is reserved for when you really mean it, as when somebody saves your life! No word, either, for "I'm sorry."

One day I asked Tiana Bighorse how this could be. She looked surprised at the question.

"Don't need the word. When you walk through a trading post and your long skirt knock cans off a shelf, if you're sorry, you pick it up. If not, you just leave it there. If you step on somebody foot, if you're sorry, you just get off."

One Thanksgiving, after we'd been in Tuba City over a year, Tiana's daughter, Sallie, and her husband came to dinner. A meal and bottle of wine later, Sallie, The-One-Who-Finesses-Both-Cultures, said, "I just want to tell you there hasn't been another Anglo who has gotten as involved in Navajo ways. The people really appreciate it. But they won't tell you; it's not their way."

"Oh, Sallie, I've been here all this time and I'm still learning real basic stuff. Here I've been going around thanking your Mom every time she teaches me anything—you know, trying to do the right thing. Now I find out it's all wrong. And I just learned there's no question-form in the Navajo language—just statement. I mean, when I want to ask a question, I'm suppose to start my statement with a "da' "-sound, or end it with "sh." Isn't that right?"

Sallie nodded.

"See, all this time your Mom's been visiting me about four in the afternoon, about the time I'm putting weaving tools away, thinking Jack's going to be home soon after five, and dinner needs to be ready at six. I'm always glad when your Mom comes. I learn a lot from her and enjoy her. We talk about weaving and family and who's sick and who's in trouble. About half an hour later she says why she's there:

'Take me to the store,' she says.

"Well, of course I can't take her to the store right then. I still have to clean up the house and thaw the meat and fix the vegetables. If I take her to the store right then, I'm going to be late. But I say, 'O.K. I'll take you to the store.'

"You know how long it takes at the trading post. Lean against the wall. Buy food. Maybe sell a rug. Talk to friends. Lean some more. Could be an hour or more. So on the way home, just as I'm thinking how to make a real quick dinner, your Mom says, 'Take me to the post office.'

"Of course, by now Jack's already home to an empty house and dinner table. But I say, 'O.K.' Getting mail can only take a second.

"After that it's 'Take me to Sallie's house.' And even if we don't stay long at your house, it's well after 6:30 when we get back to your Mom's hogan. There she just gets out of the car and walks off. Never says 'Thank You.' "

Sallie listened attentively.

"But, you know what I figured out just today? Your Mom never says thanks because she's translating Navajo into English. I'm just taking her to the store and the post office and your house. I'm not saving her life. Same way about telling me to take her different places. In her mind she's probably saying, 'Da'-Take-me-to-the-store' or 'Take-me-to-the-Post-Office-sh.' She's asking me! I have a choice. All this time I could have said, 'You know, it's not so good for me right now, but if you come back tomorrow morning, maybe around ten, I'd be glad to take you to the store.' "

Sallie nodded and smiled.

Some weeks later Tiana came to visit in the morning around ten, and sat in the chair to the right of the door, feet together, arms folded, and talked about family and who was sick and whose marriage wasn't going well. When it was time to speak of why she had come, she said simply, "I was wondering. Take me to the store."

After a time of talking, joking and trading at the post, back in the car Tiana said: "I talked to that lady in there. She say she have two rug on her loom. She makes real big one. I was wondering. Take me to her hogan."

After that weaver, there was another. And so it went until in early afternoon, while admiring some almost-finished rugs, I overheard her say in Navajo with a gesture toward me:

"I teach this bilagáana (Anglo) to weave. She weave real good. She really likes weaving stories. She don't know Navajo real good. You tell me the stories. I'll tell her."

What a considerate way to ask, I thought. She isn't asking for herself, though she too enjoys the stories. This way, if the lady declines, she will only be saying "No" to me.

The weaver began telling the sacred weaving stories to Tiana who translated them for me. I listened purely and precisely, honoring each word. Here were new legends, different versions of familiar stories, details that brought disparate tales together.

The entire day was a gift. On the way home we talked about the stories and what they might mean on deeper levels. All the while, I kept trying to figure out ways of expressing my thanks without saying "those words."

"That was a wonderful time that we had with your friend," I began . "I always enjoy hearing weaving stories . . . . Now that I heard these new stories, I understand others better."

When at last we drove up to her hogan at the end of the day, Tiana put her hand on the door handle, then suddenly reconsidered. Returning hand to lap, she turned to me,

"Well, thank you!" And walked off to her hogan.

An Old Man Came Into The Trading Post

and gestured to the Anglo sales clerk behind the counter. He pointed first to an old turquoise nugget necklace in the case and then to her. With animated gestures he was clearly trying to get her to put it on. At first she ignored him completely. But he persisted until she understood what he wanted. Still she hesitated. The necklace was the most expensive in the entire post; she was just the sales clerk; the trader wasn't there to authorize her wearing such an expensive piece. What if it broke or got stolen? Besides, it didn't go with what she had on.

Others in the post began to gather around. The reticent clerk reconsidered. Maybe it would be best to go along with the old man. Anything to quiet him down. She put on the necklace and the old man nodded and grinned and circled the group eliciting approval.

After a while, he went off to shop for food but kept returning to the clerk and the necklace. Several hours later when his English-speaking son came to pick him up, the sales clerk stopped them at the door.

"Why does your father want me to wear this necklace so much?"

"The necklace has been in the showcase maybe four months now. Before that, it was in the pawn vault. Maybe over a year. My father's been watching it. Each time he comes in, it looks worse and worse. He's afraid it isn't going to make it."

If you own turquoise, you have a responsibility to keep it healthy. When it is worn constantly, the skin and the sun warm it, and it rubs on the clothes. Its luster grows. Some of the older women say that turquoise should be washed at night in yucca and dried, then put in a bàsket of cornmeal to "feed" it. Perhaps this ritual removes body oils it has absorbed during the day. But, they add, "most people don't bother with that anymore."

I always wore my turquoise on the reservation. One particular necklace— two strands of Morenci nuggets, purchased one year at Pow Wow from a Santo Domingo medicineman — fascinated the Navajo medicinemen. On one occasion, shopping at the local

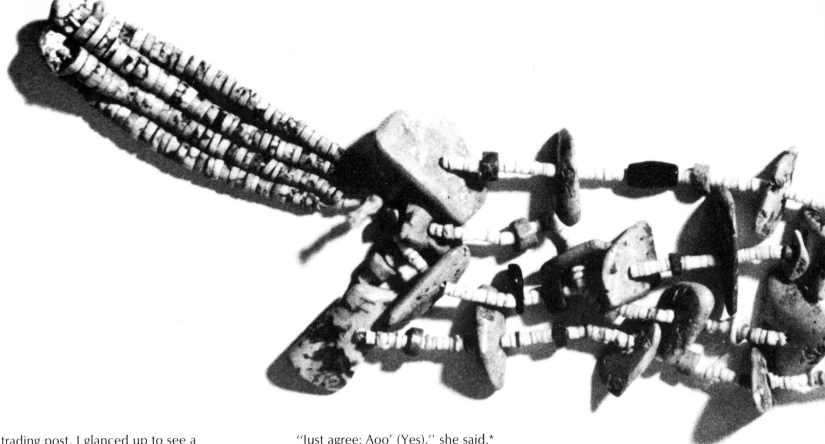

trading post, I glanced up to see a medicineman crossing the room, coming directly toward me. Grabbing the necklace (a bit roughly for my cultural conditioning), he pulled it toward him and examined it closely.

"Nizhóní! (That's beautiful!)." Then he walked away.

Eventually I understood that in the Navajo way it's all right to look openly at someone—not into their eyes directly, but at whatever they are wearing or doing. To become more comfortable in trading-post encounters, I asked Tiana Bighorse what my response should be when someone praised my jewelry.

"Just agree: Aoo' (Yes)," she said.*

At first I felt awkward concurring in praise of my necklace, but in time I came to enjoy it—even reverse it. When I would see a Navajo laden with magnificent turquoise at Pow Wow, I no longer snuck a surreptitious peek. I was free simply to walk up and look. I *really* saw the color and matrix of the stone.

"Nizhóní!"

"Aoo' "

It felt like turquoise was put there for people's pleasure. And to voice pleasure

_____

*One certainly doesn't say "Thank you!"

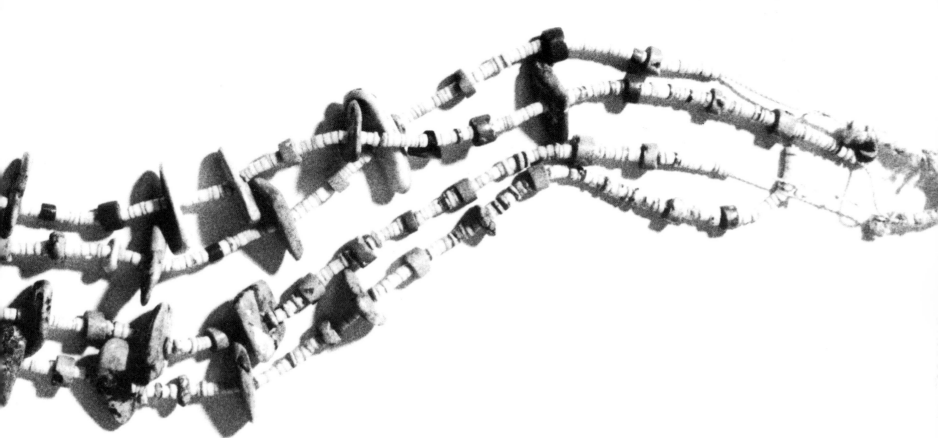

in the sight was as natural and right as breathing.

I came to understand Navajo openness about looking in other ways. We often attended all-night healing ceremonies—the only Anglos present. It seemed everytime I glanced up, people were looking at me—at my turquoise? my moccasins? my old pawn buttons? my newly made satin skirt or velvet blouse? my lighter skin? The Navajo expression revealed nothing.

Even during breaks when people talked to each other, they'd look at me and talk at the same time. I constantly wondered what they were saying.

At one ceremony I was close enough to overhear a conversation. Two women, sitting with skirts touching, were speaking quietly and looking right at me. Perhaps if I listened. Even with my Navajo, I might be able to understand at least a few words. Tuning my ear to the difficult sounds, I found I could understand the conversation.

One lady, eyes directly on me, was saying "Last week we went to Utah and picked Sonny up at the boarding school."

Her friend answered, "He'll probably be home all summer, won't he?"

The Public Health Service Compound Was A Place Set Apart.

Cyclone-fenced yards. Stuccoed boxes. Cement driveways. This was government housing. All twelve doctors at the Tuba City hospital lived there during their two-year commitment. Many encountered difficulty adjusting to life in this remote area and lamented the "lack of culture" on reservation. To endure the time, wives home during the day formed reading groups, baking groups, quilting groups. On weekends, doctors' families went four-wheeling.

When one wife asked me to show her how to weave, I gave the request some thought. I was really pleased she wanted to get involved in a native craft. But I also felt that my teaching her would be inappropriate, so I encouraged her to find a way to learn directly from a Navajo weaver. She replied that on several occasions she had tried to find one, but couldn't. Besides, she was shy. If only she knew just a little bit, she would feel more comfortable asking someone to show her more.

In the end, it was probably because she was my friend that I relented. I said I would show her just how to card the wool.

On the appointed morning, accompanied by my brother on break from the University of California, I selected some of my cleanest and most lustrous fleece, removed all manure clumps and stickers, and set off for Peggy's. I told her we would first wash the wool. I filled the sink with lukewarm water and a squirt of soap and gently began pushing the wool up and down in solution. I exclaimed about the silky fibers, the fun ahead and encouraged her to help. She was enthusiastic about beginning her weaving, and was spilling with ideas about how to find a weaver to show her more. Steam from the warm water, and the specific smell of wet wool, wafted upward as she leaned over the sink. She gagged. How could I stand it, she asked. From outside the kitchen she apologetically explained that she just couldn't abide the smell of the wool. Would I wash it for her?

No. I insisted she would have to do it herself and suggested we take it outside to wash it in a bucket of cold water.

The air was clear and cool with gentle breezes. I was confident I had solved Peggy's difficulty of the "closeness" and encouraged her to take over the washing. But as she stood over the bucket, about to plunge her hands into the sheepy water, the smell of wet wool again overcame her. Again she was unable to go on. My brother and I fished out the dripping fleece and drained the bucket. John threw the bag of wet wool over his shoulder and set out with long strides toward home.

After a while he spoke. "You know, Noël, some day you should write a book about all this. Maybe you could point out that interactions are not always easy—in fact beginnings are usually tough. Then maybe talk about what happens if you don't get past the hard parts. You never get to the Beauty.

"And," he smiled, "you could call the book, *The Smell of the Wool.*"

"She Doesn't Even Know To Use Short Pieces!"

Two old Navajo women were standing behind me talking loudly to each other in the Tuba City community center. I squirmed uncomfortably. I had been asked to judge the Miss Tuba City contest where young Navajo women annually compete in two skill categories: contemporary and traditional. The contestants were often accomplished at typing and shorthand and English language skills. But when they sat beside a rug or belt loom, or were questioned in their native tongue, they became ill at ease and flustered.

Typically, young women who entered the contest had just come home to the reservation for summer after a school year in Utah living with Mormon "foster families." Most often friends and family had persuaded them at the last minute to enter the contest. When they protested they didn't know any traditional skills, the family would rally with a crash course.

One beautiful contestant dressed in traditional satin skirt and velvet blouse had just seated herself before her loom.

Her first action was to take a piece of yarn from the ball—a yard long.

"She doesn't even know to use short pieces!"

The words carried through the auditorium, eliciting a ripple of laughter. The contestant blushed and broke the piece in half. I shifted uneasily in my chair. What could they say if they saw me weaving?

Days later at my own loom, when I reached for the ball of yarn, I remembered the old lady's words. I broke the precise length from the ball and slid it into the shed.

I was uncomfortable everytime I encountered ridicule in the Navajo culture. Here was blunt reversal of how I had been raised and had raised my children. Yet I wanted to understand and accept it within the Navajo context. I could see it was an effective means of teaching. But how about when it was used to motivate someone who lagged behind or squelch someone who tried to excel? I wondered why individuality was seen as detrimental.

There is strength in unity. So perhaps Navajo survival depends upon conformity. Not only must they survive against the elements, but the Navajo must also hold onto their traditions against a worse threat, white marauders seeking to change their ways.

"She doesn't even know to use short pieces."

While carding: "She doesn't even know to keep her arm straight."

While weaving: "She doesn't even know to keep the fork in her hand. Let's just chase her away from here."

Jewelry Bedecked The Ears, Necks, Fingers, Wrists And Waists

of patrons seeking the ultimate collectible. It was opening night at the annual Museum of Northern Arizona Navajo Show. And it was packed! Jewelry, pottery, baskets and rugs layered in profusion. Blue and red ribbons signaled the ultimate in fine craftsmanship or innovative design.

As I wandered among the textiles, absorbed in their rich, muted colors, I was impressed that the rugs Helen Tsinnie and Tiana Bighorse wove were as well crafted as these. Here traders and collectors had selected the best of their stock for the show. The museum had awarded ribbons, comparing each piece to an absolute standard—not against each other. At show-end, the ribbon stayed with the rug to validate the collection. It didn't even go to the woman who had made it. Most often, the weaver wouldn't even know her rug had been entered—much less won a prize.

I thought there should be a way for the individual weaver to enter the museum show. When I asked the staff whether traditional craftsmen ever entered their own pieces, they said it was rare, even though the museum encouraged it. I could see that the imposing museum setting, the predominance of English-speaking people and Anglo customs could be frightening deterrents.

Months after the show, I kept thinking that if either Tiana or Helen could finish a rug in time for next year, I would take it to the museum and enter it for them. I told them my idea and asked them to think about it.

The idea of entering a museum show seemed foreign to Tiana, but she gave it her usual open consideration. She was used to weaving a rug for money, not for prizes. If it were put in the show, she wouldn't be paid right away as she would if she sold it to a trader. (Entries had to be submitted a month early. Money from sales during the month-long show was disbursed at the end.) Then there was the matter of finishing by a certain date. Many things came up during the course of a rug: ceremonies, sickness, babysitting, trips. A rug was done when it was done.

One of her family suggested, in good

Navajo humor, that if I wanted so much to enter a rug why didn't I enter mine?! I laughed and explained that this was a *Navajo* Arts and Crafts show and that entries had to be Navajo. They laughed and exclaimed that no one would know the difference—I had hand-spun, plant-dyed and woven the yarn exactly as their mother had taught me. In fact, entering it would be a good joke. Could those Anglo museums who knew everything about Indians tell the difference? I protested that my first and only rug was still on the loom and that it was obviously a beginner piece—the spinning was erratic, the edges were woven unevenly, especially at the beginning. I had incorporated so many different designs in order to learn the various Navajo techniques, it didn't even look typically Navajo. It was a learning sampler; entering it was out of the question.

Instead of dropping the subject, the group batted it with greater and greater momentum about the family circle. Someone asked rhetorically if, when their mother had woven on my Anglo loom, using pedals attached to heddles to work on my Anglo design, had she in fact been making a Navajo rug because she was Navajo? Another asked what I thought I had been weaving all this time on the Navajo loom in the middle of the reservation—a Persian rug? Another round of laughter: everyone knew about my father's middle-eastern heritage.

Months later I talked to Helen Tsinnie. Since several Public Health Service doctors owned her Yei tapestries, there was no problem getting pieces to enter. I would need to check with the museum and make sure it was all right to enter a rug in the show that wasn't for sale. Her tapestries would be entered for prize only, and the ribbon would go to her. She was delighted with the idea and suggested I enter mine, too. She sounded just like Tiana's family.

Besides the humor of the semantics, my friends really wanted to see if they had taught me well by Anglo museum standards. Perhaps an unstated, unconscious aspect of the humor was also that entering my rug would place me squarely in a bind between cultures. With my academic background I clearly understood the "ethics" and "prestige" of the museum. Being now immersed in Navajo Way, I was equally taken by the Navajo fun-poking at pretentiousness. Without committing myself to yes or no, I promised to write the museum for entry rules.

When the official museum letter finally came I took it to Tiana's home to read aloud. It began:

> Thank you for your interest in the 1970 Museum of Northern Arizona annual Navajo Arts and Crafts show. In answer to your questions regarding entry requirements, all entries:
>
> 1. Must have been woven on an upright Navajo loom using traditional Navajo techniques.
> 2. Must have a Navajo census number.
> 3. Need not be for sale.

The letter concluded that pieces must be brought to the museum by a specific date, less than a month away; it was signed by the director.

"Well, that finishes that," I exclaimed to Sallie, who was visiting her mother. "I can't enter my rug because I don't have a Navajo census number."

"I have a Navajo census number," she said. "I'll give it to the piece. It doesn't say the weaver needs one—just the piece!"

The rest of the family whooped it up about this good joke on the Anglo museum system with its rules and regulations and anthropologic insistence upon "studying" the Indian. Before the evening was over, it was all decided.

Soon I made the trek to Flagstaff with weavings in the back of the jeep. Tiana had not finished one in time, but I had borrowed two of Helen's from a doctor-friend. "Now, I'm not going to lie," I vowed to myself. I was willing to play this Navajo game, but I'd keep my integrity.

On past visits to the museum I had often questioned the validity of the sign hanging above the entrance:

> This Museum displays ideas, not things.

Today, walking through with my pile of "Navajo" rugs, the sign's staid position provoked a further twinge. I wondered if there was anyone inside this archeological/anthropological institution who would enjoy the cross-cultural humor of this "idea," should my charade be discovered. I seriously doubted it.

Inside, I carried the roll of rugs to a lady sitting at a table next to a stack of papers. I patted Helen Tsinnie's beautiful mohair Yei tapestry atop my pile.

"I'd like to enter these rugs in the show." I felt the terseness of my own words, the stiffness of my back. My arms, I suddenly noticed, were folded. In this Anglo world I was acting strangely Navajo. I flashed on body language books I had read. In the Anglo culture, my stance was supposed to indicate "hostility" and "insecurity." I held the position.

"Well, we're glad that so many people are bringing rugs in this year," the accessioner said to me as she shuffled her papers without looking up.

"About as many entries this year as before?" I asked. I was monitoring every word that came out of my mouth for its Truth.

"Actually, there are even more entries than ever. In fact, the museum has had to make a few changes from years past. First, everyone's pieces will not automatically be hung. Since there are so many pieces, we're just going to display the most unusual."

If that's the criteria, they ought to love mine! I thought, picturing the twill, two-face, snake and roadrunner. "I can understand that. You have to select pieces that make up the best show as a whole."

"Yes, and with so many entries it's going to be quite a job," the museum person continued. "We've had to apply another new rule this year. We've had so many complaints in years past that some of the best pieces weren't available for purchase. This year, *all* pieces must be for sale."

I was aghast. Sell my one and only weaving? Never! I was woven into that piece! Additionally, the weavings I had brought of Helen Tsinnie's were from

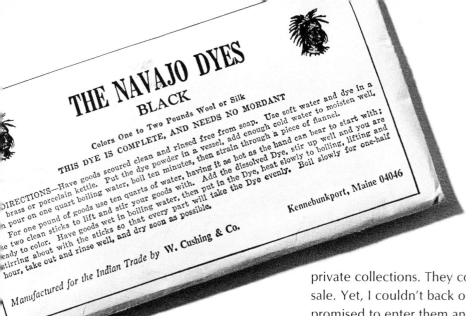

private collections. They couldn't be for sale. Yet, I couldn't back out; I had promised to enter them and was intent on making this Museum-Of-Ideas acknowledge her ability with a prize.

I reached into my purse and pulled out the letter. "You know, I wrote to the museum several months ago asking the criteria for entering. They told me that entries didn't have to be for sale, just woven on a Navajo loom with a Navajo census number. I just drove all the way from Tuba City to bring these rugs and *none* of them is for sale."

The lady stopped measuring the weaving. She adjusted her bifocals, and carefully read the letter including the signature. A moment later she was on the phone to the director and very soon he appeared. He assured the accessioner that in this instance the museum would have to accept the pieces since the letter had predated the museum decision.

Personnel were now gathering about

the table, and I felt the wishes of my Navajo friends back on reservation growing dimmer. I reconsidered entering my weaving. It was safely buried at the bottom of my pile. Maybe I could unobtrusively sneak it out.

Dealers with rugs to enter were now backing up behind me. The accessioner, having been directed to accept my entries, finished measuring the first piece and began the questions:

"Weaver's name?"

"Helen Tsinnie."

"Kinds of dyes."

"Plant."

"Area of reservation?"

"Tuba City."

The lady took the rug, attached the appropriate identification, and stacked it neatly on another table. She began measuring the next:

"Weaver's name?"

"Same"

"Kind of dyes?"

"Same."

"Area of the reservation?"

"Same."

Again she attached identification to the weaving.

My own piece had now surfaced. I was preparing to snatch it off the pile while she was stacking Helen's last rug, but the lady broke her routine to examine the tufting in the center of my sampler.

"Never seen one like this!" She numbered her page and my entry and placed both mine and Helen Tsinnie's rug on the accessioned stack, having neither measured nor questioned mine. "Of course, even though we accept these pieces, you understand they won't necessarily be hung," she reminded me. "We'll only be hanging the best."

I nodded, eyeing the uneven edges of my coarsely woven beginner piece. I was stunned by the suddenness with which my one and only weaving had disappeared into the masses. Numbly I turned and headed back to the reservation.

I didn't have the courage to go to the opening's preview. But, feeling like a criminal returning to the scene of the crime, I visited the museum early one morning after the show had been up for several weeks. As in past shows, the atrium was spilling over with beautiful rugs. By now I was sure my rug, with its beginner mistakes, wouldn't be among them. That was actually a relief, but I was still eager to see Helen Tsinnie's prizes. It took quite a while amidst the heavy layering of textiles to locate her pieces, but both had the blue ribbons I had envisioned! My sampler was decidedly not there.

I wandered about the museum enjoying the rest of the show. In an adjoining room I looked through cases of Navajo jewelry. As in other years, the craftsmanship was superb and I tested myself—guessing the kind of turquoise and the craftsman's name before reading the label.

The next room, in contrast to the past two, was spacious with artwork sparsely displayed. A full-sized ceremonial sandpainting was roped off in the middle of the floor. Very few items hung on the walls: a few skeins of yarn, some Navajo wedding baskets, a few Navajo weaving tools. And one more object directly opposite me at eye level. My weaving.

I felt a warm flush sweep up through shoulders, neck and face. I wanted to rush to it, and whoop in joy at seeing it displayed there in the museum. I thought of the fun it would be to tell my weaving mentors about it. I also wanted to turn and run. Right next to the lower right corner was a small white sign. The ultimate horror flashed before me. Probably my weaving had been so isolated in order to teach a well-deserved lesson. The sign was probably in capital letters:

THIS IS A FAKE NAVAJO RUG.

Uneasily I walked over to the much-too-familiar weaving and bent to read the small sign: "Small Native Dye. Tuba City." I looked back at the weaving and then sat down on a bench at roomside to sort through the meaning. All the other signs had weavers' names. But on this piece, the accessioner hadn't taken that information. Then I noticed a red ribbon tied to the bottom corner tassel.

At that moment, a visitor spotted the only weaving in the room and stepped in front of me to see it better. She looked at each of the weaving bands of different techniques, then at the sign. "Small Native Dye. Tuba City." She looked back at the weaving. The sun-design buried in tufting apparently intrigued her. She smoothed it out with her fingers as though touch would help her integrate the piece with her concept of Navajo weaving. It didn't. She looked back at the label for further explanation. "Small Native Dye. Tuba City." She shrugged and moved on.

A docent came into the room. I gathered courage and went over to her. "I've been looking at this unusual weaving. I wonder, can you tell me something about it?"

She eyed me with a tinge of exasperation. "Don't ask me about that piece. Everyone has been asking me about that piece. The sign just says 'Small Native Dye. Tuba City.' " She paused, brushing the grey tufting away from the sun-design as the lady before her had. "But, if you ask me, it's a cross between a Navajo and a Persian."

One day
as you sit and weave
you may muse on warp and weft:
how they mesh their essences,
how they fuse their strengths.

Warp
so taut
so hard
so straight
so tightly spun
so tightly strung.
It shapes the whole.
Holds the course.
Innerstrength
unseen.

Weft conversely is soft and supple.
Gently yielding.
Textured.
Mellow.
Envelops the warp as it twines.
Buffers the core; creates design.

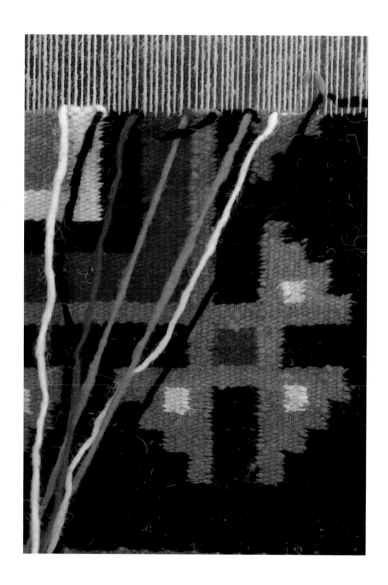

Thus, as always,
two unite.

Opposites
form a whole—
The basis for creativity
the foundation
for all of life.

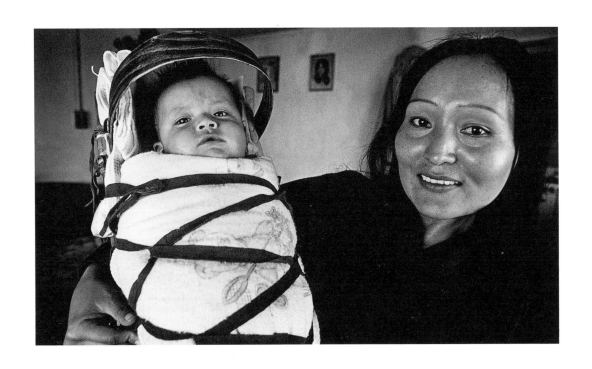

Garlic, Oregano, Basil And Garden Tomatoes Had Been Simmering Since Noon.

By 6:00 PM the water was boiling for noodles. This time it was the real thing.

Spaghetti for dinner had become a household joke. Many times, Jack, home from the hospital, had come directly into the kitchen to check boiling pots on the stove. "Spaghetti!" It was his favorite dish. But then, moments later, as he stirred the pot, what appeared to be noodles transformed into yarn. Handspun fleece, bubbling in a sea of mountain mahogany, red-barked juniper, Navajo tea.

But this evening, dye pots had been scoured and stored and even the everpresent manuscript had been put away for the night. I continued to neaten the house, and the clock edged toward 6:30. Jack was now an hour later than usual. At 6:45 I considered walking the short distance to the hospital on chance we would meet halfway and stroll back together.

But I arrived at the hospital without seeing him. Should I go in? I wouldn't know where to look in the labyrinth of hospital halls. Just then, through the door

window, I caught sight of him in conference with a Navajo nurse. I went in and told him dinner was ready.

The nurse hardly looked up. Conversations without eye-contact were the Navajo way. She changed the subject to something about the fourth floor of the hospital. Knowing nothing about the medical or hospital world, I didn't follow the discussion. Instead, I thought about the Angloness of my own actions. Dinner ready for the husband at 6:00 was directly contradictory to traditional Navajo way. On reservation, women prepared food at their own convenience. If the man was hungry, he hung around, and "got his legs under the table" at the right time. The Navajo ladies always giggled at the way I catered to Jack's schedule.

The nurse was now looking at me but talking to Jack. "Dr. Bennett, you really ought to be up on the fourth floor."

"We're just on our way home—dinner's ready." Jack turned to go. We had fully descended the outside steps when a different Navajo nurse called out to us.

"Coming down from the fourth floor,

Dr. Bennett?"

Something was clearly going on. In unison we turned and headed back the way we had come.

Sign on the door: "Fourth Floor. Maternity Ward." Chanting wafting faintly down the sterile hall. We followed the sound. A small room. In the middle, a young Navajo woman in bed. Obviously pregnant. Obviously in labor. Around her several women. Mother? Grandmother? Sisters? Concerned faces. No sound except the chanting of the medicineman.

The beat began to quicken. The singer reached into his pouch and sprinkled corn pollen. He brought out a large skein of white "store bought" yarn, held it firmly in his left hand and with his right, formed a circle. Then he reached in and pulled through a section of the skein further down, forming a new loop. Loop after loop after loop. He was, in effect, hand-crocheting. Chaining a kind of knot.

This jumble of yarn he held over the patient's belly, chanting and pulling. Chanting and pulling. The chain almost imperceptibly elongated. Unraveling. Unraveling for perhaps five minutes, until

at last the skein was fully free of the clump, and the chant ended.

I stood watching. Senses open. Back straight, arms folded, feet together in the Navajo format. What was going on?

At the end of the chant, the medicineman began talking with the mother. I didn't bother to listen. Certainly with my limited vocabulary, I wouldn't understand. But, the conversation intensified and they began looking about the room. I tuned my ear to the words. One sound only was recognizable. "Tó."

Water! They were talking about water. Taking a chance on a liberal interpretation, I told Jack, in English, they wanted some water. The Navajos seemed surprised to hear my voice. Jack had a look of distrust. Did he think my speaking disruptive? Was he questioning how I knew?

"They want some water. Get them some."

Silently Jack fetched some and offered it in a basin. The medicineman gratefully took it. The old lady looked at me and smiled, then moved next to me. I felt she was validating my being there.

The chanting started up again and I set my mind to unraveling the meaning. I thought back. Three times we had been told to come—the first seemed to be elicited by my showing up. The patient was pregnant. I recalled various weavers teasing me, asking me if *I* was pregnant. No, not now. But what if I were? Then I should tie all my knots as square knots or bows—ones that come undone easily. Not only that, I should finish my rug before the baby came.

One weaver had explained that if the rug was unfinished, the baby might be born with the umbilical cord wrapped about its neck. But finishing off the rug untied all knots unassociated with the rug itself—a symbolic release of the cord. Understanding was close. And then I remembered. The word, at'ló, "to knot",

is the same as "to weave."

So, unchaining the skein of yarn over the womb might symbolically untie knots from both loom and cord.

Clarity collided with silence. The second chant had ended. I leaned toward the woman beside me, and nodded toward the patient. In threadbare Navajo I whispered "Is this your daughter, my mother?"

"Aoo'."(Yes.)

"This baby. Your daughter's first?"

"Aoo'."

I paused and took a breath. Should I proceed? I had to know! "Is your daughter a weaver, my mother?"

"Aoo'."

"Did your daughter finish her rug?"

"Dooda!" (No!)

Tónaneesdizí—Tangled Waters—Tuba City.

It is a Mormon-made town with cottonwoods lining the straight main street. It was named by its founders after Chief Tuba, but the Navajo continue to use the name that celebrates water in the desert.

People gather around water, so many reservation places contain the syllable "Tó":

Tuba City (tónaneesdizí): "Tangled-Waters"

Kaibito (k'ai' bii' tó): "Willows-About-the-Water"

Dinebito (diné bito'): "The People—their Water"

Iyanbito ('ayání bito'): "Buffalo-Springs"

Shonto (shááďóhí): "Where-The-Sunlight-Hits-The-Water"

Tuba is at 4000' elevation; Shonto is at 8000'. In the desert, the higher you are, the more water there is and therefore the greener it is. Shonto seemed like an oasis to us. After living in Tuba for two years, we considered moving to this remote location.

Shonto had never had a full-time doctor. No doctors wanted to live "that far from civilization," or to subject their children to "the poor educational experience." But we thought we would find worthwhile life experiences in Shonto. Jack felt a professional concern as well. The Navajo living in the expanses between there and the Utah border had a half-day's pick-up drive to the nearest Public Health Service medical facility. Jack thought Shonto should be a triage center. He could treat people who didn't require hospitalization and send the more serious cases on to larger facilities, an hour's drive farther.

All of us went through changes when we moved to Shonto. None of us could rely on English. Jack, who was seeing up to sixty patients a day, needed a nurse-interpreter to help him; I had to find new weavers and continue my learning now almost completely in Navajo.

Shawn, too, was affected. He was attending second grade in Kayenta, an hour-and-a-half bus ride morning and night. Since his classes were taught in English, by Anglo teachers, academic life was easy. But he was the only Anglo in his class, an exceedingly small minority of one. At the end of the first school quarter, I went to a parent-teacher meeting. I wanted to hear how Shawn was doing.

"I just want you to know I have never seen an Anglo child as well-accepted as Shawn," the teacher began. I was pleased. I asked her if she thought it might be because Shawn had been around a lot of my weaving friends. Or perhaps his athletic abilities made him a good teammate.

"That probably helps," she said. "But it's more than that. It has to do with his sense of humor." She offered an example.

"At the beginning of the year, when Shawn first showed up at school, the Navajo kids followed him around chanting: 'Blue-eye. Blue-eye. Blue-eye. Blue-eye.' "

I smiled. The Navajo loved to name a person's most obvious characteristic—for Shawn, his intensely blue eyes. And for the black-haired, black-eyed, pun-loving Navajo, the name served double-duty to target his Angloness. Good name.

"In second grade kids don't like to

stand out," the teacher went on. "They like to be a part of the group. So Shawn didn't like it when the Navajo kids followed him around chanting. At first he told them, 'I don't like it when you call me, "Blue-eye." ' But they kept it up.

"You know most Navajos are shorter than most Anglos, and Shawn's tall for his age anyway—the tallest in the class. I could see the chanting really bothered him but he was trying not to show it. Maybe he was just biding his time.

"One morning one of the largest Navajo boys was at him again: 'Blue-Eye. Blue-eye. Blue-eye.' Shawn looked around the playground. All the kids were watching to see what he would do. Slowly he drew himself up to his fullest height, placed his fist near the guy's face and hollered,

'You call me "Blue-Eye" one more time, and I'll call you "Black-And-Blue-Eye!" ' That ended that."

Two years later Shawn discovered that all the Navajo kids in his fourth grade had a Navajo name except him. One evening when he was talking about feeling left out, I reminded him he had had a Navajo name, but had discouraged it. But now, he suggested, maybe Tiana Bighorse could give him another. Would I ask her?

The next time I went to visit, I spoke for Shawn in Navajo way. Without going into the story about Shawn's first Navajo name, I simply told her Shawn wanted her to name him. Tiana said she would give it thought and talk to her family. Several months later she announced their decision. Shawn's name would be "Ashkiiłtsoii"—"Golden Boy."

She explained. "We name him for his lightness. He has light skin and blond hair. But the main thing, he has very blue eyes."

The Mercury Dropped—Twenty Degrees Below Zero.

Not unusual for a Shonto winter. I got into bed, grateful for my down comforter.

But suddenly the ringing doorbell awakened me. I looked at the clock—it was 2 AM. I tied my robe about me and stumbled to the door. On the porch, a man and woman. Arms folded. Hands tucked tightly under jacket armpits. Shoulders hunched up against the cold.

"I want to see the doctor." The man spoke in broken English.

I invited them inside.

"What do you need?" Jack came into the living room.

"I stepped on a nail."

"When?" Even in his sleep Jack habitually took case histories.

"Maybe a month ago."

Things didn't make sense, this man appearing in the middle of the night for less than a medical emergency. Jack explained he didn't have medical tools at the house; they should go to the medical station and Jack would dress and meet them there.

The couple made no motion to leave, so Jack repeated his directive; perhaps they hadn't understood. Still they waited.

"Is there something else you wanted?"

"Yes." This time the woman spoke. "We haven't seen your wife weave."

A weaving begins in joy.

The warp is long and strong.
The weft is full and supple.

The two combine.
The two entwine.

And thus the loom conceives.

Days dawn, replete with promise.

Months pass, flushed with grace.

Gaining.
Growing.
Spreading.
Swelling.
Life and loom fulfill their own.

Then comes the time of fruited fullness.
Then comes the time of bearing ripeness,
when the weaving slackens pace.
For the loom now is heavy with rug
and the space to weave is close
and tight.

Deep Winter. The Fry-Bread Flour Sack Is Empty.

White snowdrifts stack high outside the hogan. Inside, a family of eight circles the wood stove staving off the cold. The route to the trading post is impassable; children are hungry; there's nothing to do but wait out the storm.

Grandfather reaches into a special pouch and carefully withdraws—a *string*. Slowly he wraps it about his hands, then with increasing rapidity chains it through his fingers—flipping loops, drawing lengths. So begins the complex designs known as Navajo string games, an activity sanctioned only in the season after the first snow and before spring, when spiders and snakes are asleep.

One set of complicated motions ends in a sudden snapped gesture. A loose double string flips into a zig-zag. "Lightning!" Grandfather's enjoyment shows in his toothless grin. Pulling just the right strand, the whole configuration instantly disappears, leaving the children wondering at the flash.

Again the string begins its journey, around the little finger of the left hand, picked up by the thumb, interlaced over-and-under cross strands. The right hand holds the formation out to display a long loose loop stretching across the string terrain. The right hand starts its undulation, setting the attenuated loop into motion. Slowly it slithers, tracing a zig-zag path. It becomes smaller and smaller, then seeps into a crack by the thumb and is gone: "Snake-Going-Into-A-Hole!"

Grandfather sits very straight; the hogan is quiet now. Children lean forward, intent on the world he weaves between his hands. Seemingly through a spiderweb of cross-strings and tangles, fingers unerringly seek the right strands until across the taut network, two cross-loops appear. Both hands slowly gyrate. The loops begin to separate, to glide toward opposite sides of creation. "Two Coyotes Running Apart."

"Tell us the story about Coyote!"
"Yes, Coyote!"

Then perhaps on that snowy day, with food supply low, Grandfather may tell a Coyote story. For the intriguing character of Coyote is everyone's favorite. He is Fool and Trickster. He is also Wiseman.

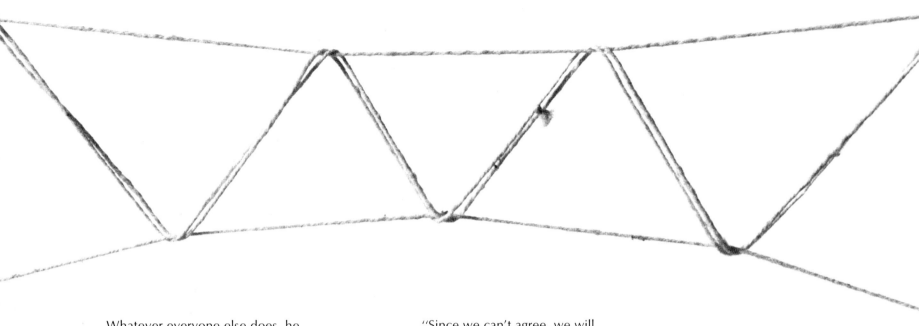

Whatever everyone else does, he cavalierly undermines. His actions are startling. And only later, somewhat begrudgingly, we acknowledge their rightness.

First Man, First Woman and the First Beings are discussing Death. Everyone agrees that people should live forever and never die. Only in this way can experience and wisdom compound.

Coyote alone dissents. "There must be Death. Limited time is essential to Life. Without Death, Life has no meaning."

They debate the subject earnestly and persistently until a stalemate is reached. Coyote speaks up again.

"Since we can't agree, we will throw two stones into the water. If one floats, there shall be death."

First Man and First Woman heartily agree. They know stones don't float! Immediately they throw theirs into the water, watch it sink and rejoice triumphantly. Then Coyote readies his. But instead of a stone, he picks up a piece of wood that looks exactly like stone. Into the water he tosses it—and it floats.

That is why there is Death. Jiní; so it is said.

As Grandfather ends his story he resumes his string. He knows the importance of silence in story telling. The trickster quality of Coyote must be mulled. It is essential that Coyote win, not through fair play but by cleverness.

Now the fingers play out the rhythms of the star formations: Horned-Star, Big Star, Many Stars. And the story of how the stars were put in the sky is remembered and told.

The Gods agree that stars should be put in the sky in precise clusters to remind those on the earth plane below of important life lessons. Because of Coyote's bumptiousness, the Gods decide not to tell him what they are going to do. On the prearranged night, they secretly bring out the star pouch, and carefully create each cluster. They put one star-cluster to mark the time to hunt, and one to mark the time to plant. They also put a male constellation, Hastiin Sik'aii. And a female constellation, Seven Sisters (Pleiedes). They arrange things so these two constellations will never be visible simultaneously. When Hastiin is up, the Pleiedes are down, and vise versa. In this way people will always remember that son and mother-in-law should never be present at the same time.

Just as almost all the stars are set, along comes Coyote. He is angry at not having been invited. He grabs the star pouch and looks inside. Not much left—just one big piece and lots of little crumbs. Irritated, he grabs the big piece and ceremonially plunks it in the north sky, loudly proclaiming "From now on, this great brightness will be known as Coyote Star. Unlike all others, it will not move and will guide people forevermore."

Then in a final angry act, Coyote hurls the pouch across the sky. A million star fragments spill out. "Many Stars." The Milky Way.

Perhaps randomness is essential to Perfect Order.

Slowly
the labor begins.
Deliberately
the cycle creeps to its completion.
Time is no more the precious essence.
Sun and moon no more heed course.
In an epoch of space suspended,
twixt Father Sky and Mother Earth suspended,
bearing down upon the web
the final rows
are placed.

And then
the universal joy of it all:
the freeing
releasing
unwinding of twining.
Of and through the loom it comes.
By and from a weaver's toil
a part of the structure
a piece of the maker.

Behold, the entity!
Separate
and at once
complete.

Each rug—an entity alone.
Each rug—a part of a flow.

Progeny of the past.
Forebearer of the future.

Inherent in each
the seed of the new—

As my mother
to me
now
to you.

"How Far's Your Rug?" They Glanced At My Bulging Belly.

I had run into some of my weaver friends at the Shonto Trading Post. I shook hands with each and gave assurances that the rug was almost finished.

I was in my ninth month of pregnancy. I had determined to follow Navajo pregnancy taboos. Five months ago I had started a new rug. The prototype was a Navajo design from the early 1900s with strong Persian influences. But I didn't want to just copy it. I wanted to enlarge the idea, to make a design that would honor both Navajo and Anglo tradition. And I wanted it to have personal meaning, to symbolize my body growing a second child. I began by doubling the image and augmenting the womb-like concentricity of the shapes. Then I chose the colors: mountain mahogany and indigo. Could pink and blue be done as art?

During the last five months, I had also been working, with some urgency, on a manuscript. "If the book is not completed before the baby, it may never be," I told myself. But, my pregnancy was nearing the end, and my weaver friends were more concerned for *my* safety. "The rug must be finished and off the loom before the baby is born."

Shawn had been born at the Stanford Hospital in the early sixties when Jack was a medical student. I had talked the obstetrician into natural childbirth, for I staunchly believed in the method. Now, thirteen years later, in the middle of the reservation, I intended the same. I had also intended to do daily pregnancy exercises. But, here I was at the delivery date with manuscript complete, the weaving two inches from the top, and the childbirth book unopened.

I turned my attention to my weaving. I was now at the toughest part. Here, at the end, space was tight and progress slow. In the beginning I wove six inches an hour; now it took me six hours to weave an inch. Only by sitting tailor fashion could I find comfort and space for my belly which rested on my thighs. "Keep a straight back for White Shell Woman," I heard Navajo elders advising. "It must be completed before the baby," I echoed. Row after row I lifted my arms shoulder-height to insert the batten, and the words of the Navajo chant entwined my ending:

With Beauty Before Me, It Is Woven
With Beauty Behind Me, It Is Woven
With Beauty Above Me, It Is Woven
With Beauty Below Me, It Is Woven
And In Beauty, It Is Finished.

Two weeks past my due date I took my
completed weaving off the loom. The
textile now seemed a bit of a miracle—
like it had woven itself. I hung it where I
could enjoy it, but I couldn't concentrate.
Something was wrong. My manuscript and
rug were now fully completed and here I
was, all ready to deliver. But, I hadn't
begun my exercises. I got out the book
and began to read:

"Sit tailor fashion," it began. "Keeping
back straight, raise arms shoulder height."

I felt a knowing flush. All through the
weaving of the rug, I had been physically
preparing for birth.

Weavers Told Me Not To Leave My Batten In The Loom.

So whenever I got up from weaving, I'd take it out. In time, pulling the worn oak weaving tool out of the warp and sliding it into its storage pouch began to feel like a rite of reverence. With years of use, the patinaed batten was becoming an extension of me.

One day a weaver said it again: "Never leave your batten in the loom." Then she added: "If you do, you'll never finish your rug."

Perhaps there was more to the taboo than I had thought. Maybe, left in the loom, the batten was accessible to the careless children and everpresent puppies of a normal crowded hogan. If it got used as a toy and broken, or chewed by a puppy, another tool would have to be fashioned. The weaving would certainly be delayed. From then on, when I was done, I found myself saying: "Here's to the finishing of my rug." The idea of positive conditioning within a craft made good sense to me.

One day I was sitting with Tiana Bighorse in a "ten-day project," part of the tribe's promotion of Navajo weaving on reservation. Not enough women were doing it—women could make more as secretaries. There was fear the tradition was dying out. For ten days, ten women would come to a chapter house to card, spin and dye. Prepare the wool. Then, for the next ten days, ten more would come to weave. For this they received minimum wage and the tribe would later auction the rugs, often at a loss.*

This particular day I was sitting quietly with Tiana, appreciating the opportunity to watch her and many other weavers. Each had slightly different ways of weaving, and I was learning a lot just observing. Midmorning, the lady in front of me got up and walked off, leaving her batten in the loom. The sight of the batten, left where it was not supposed to

---

*Weaving is labor intensive in any culture. So, hourly compensation is a significant improvement over selling to a post or gallery. One windless, light-filled day, my mother and I sat outside with our cleanest, silkiest wool and most balanced spindle. With stopwatch in hand we each went at our respective carding and spinning. At the end of the hour, we calculated our yarn productivity. We had jointly earned twenty-five cents.

be, jolted me. I almost blurted something outloud in alarm. But I restrained myself and stayed silent.

The lady was just starting out the door when another weaver near her said quietly, "Nimásání!" The lady whirled around, returned to her loom, and briskly removed the batten. *Then* she walked out.

I knew from Lesson One, "Nimásání" means "your grandmother."

So! Leaving a batten in the loom and not finishing a rug, had something to do with "your grandmother."

Months later, I was sitting with an English-speaking weaver. Her flow of words was keeping pace with her designs. I asked if there was anything I should know to be a good weaver.

"If you're going to be a good weaver, just don't leave your batten in the loom."

I told her I was careful not to, but I didn't exactly understand why I was supposed to take it out.

"Have you ever heard strange sounds coming from your loom?" Her voice grew soft and confidential. I felt I was being trusted, but wasn't quite certain what she meant. "Have you ever been away from your loom, and heard the sound of weaving, and when you looked no one was there?" she clarified.

"I haven't heard anything," I replied simply, feeling apologetic and certainly insensitive.

"One day I was outside working with some plants." She picked up her pace now, shoving wefts through the warp strings and beating them more loudly and quickly than before. "I was outside and I heard the sound of weaving coming from my loom. And I came back and nobody was there. I asked my daughter, 'Were you weaving on my loom?' And she said no. And I asked my other daughter, and she said no, too." She slowed her pace and looked at me out of the corner of her eye as though deciding whether to continue. "And I knew I heard that weaving on the loom."

She stopped to take a sticker out of her yarn, then pulled out the jumbled fibers and respun the section. She glanced at me before continuing her story.

"So I asked an old lady who lived in the area and she said, 'It's your grandmother. Your grandmother was a

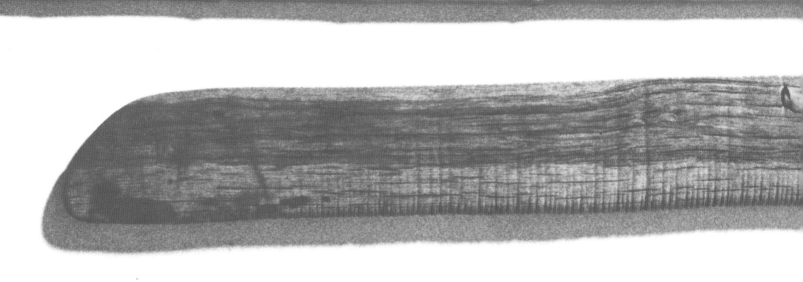

very good weaver and she wants to help you weave. But since your grandmother is dead, and the dead do everything in reverse, instead of weaving, she is unraveling!' "

There was the connection I had sought. Now things made sense, and I thought I understood.

One day I brought up the subject of traditional weaving ideas with Helen Tsinnie, weaver of the fine Yei tapestries.

"You have to be a courageous weaver to be a Yei weaver," she began. "If the Yeis don't want you to weave it, they'll let you know. Also, once you start on the head [of the Yei], you have to finish it the same day.

"Then about the batten," she continued. "One day I was sitting in my house weaving. Sitting right next to the door. Weaving on my loom. I was at the very top of my rug—past the Yei figures. You know the place where it's hard to put the batten in?"

"Yes." I knew it well.

"There I was right in that place. It takes the batten a long time to go all across the row. In that hard part, right in the middle of a row, there is a knock at my door. Well, I'm just weaving by the door, I don't even have to get up. So I just reach over and open the door. It's my relatives. They want me to come to the sheep camp. Help them shear the sheep.

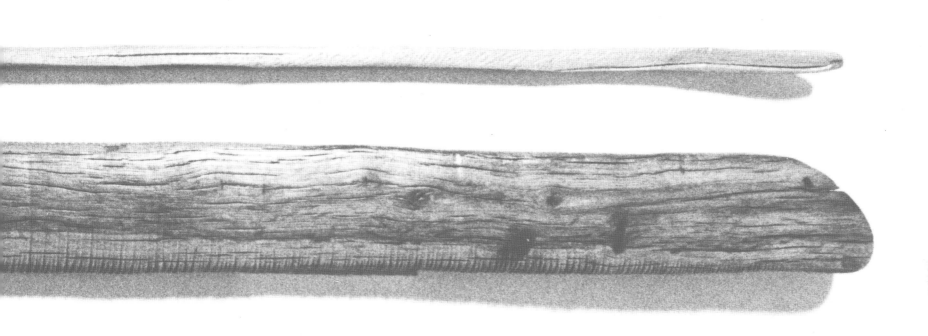

Somebody got to do the cooking. Somebody got to help with the shearing.

"I told them I can come. So I get all my things together, into my pickup, and drive to their camp. All weekend I help them. When the weekend's over I drive back home. Just before I get there, I notice a strange feeling right down the back of my neck. Like needles pricking me. It goes down the [right] side of my neck. It goes along my [right] shoulder here. And down the back of this arm. And into my back. My back really hurt and I think about it and I don't understand. I didn't do heavy work at the sheep camp. Not lift anything heavy to make my back hurt like that.

"Then, I get to my house and unload the pickup. I have to bring all my things inside. I just bring them inside and go past the loom. And there I see it. The batten is still in the loom. Right where I left it." Her voice took on a whiny, nasal sound that emphasized her trauma in seeing it. "You see, I had been weaving all weekend, and I didn't get any farther."

She was quiet and I thought about what she was saying. Then she continued.

"You see, the weaver and the loom are one. The weaver needs a rest, and the loom needs a rest. And if you leave the batten in [the loom] and go to sleep, you will never sleep good. And if you go to eat, you will never be satisfied."

"You Can Always Tell Those Who Spiritually Care About Their Weaving—Their Loomspace Is Clear All Around,"

Tiana Bighorse told me in 1970. The weaver and loom are one. What affects one, affects both.

Everything around gets woven into the rug. Wisps of yarn left lying about are caught and woven in. Loose hair from brushing floats about and is woven in. The weaver stops to remove them. The weaving rhythm is halted. The interruption is woven in.

Charles Loloma, *Hopi* silversmith, quotes his weaver-father: "It's not enough to weave beautiful rugs. You have to think beautiful thoughts while weaving them."*

An angry weaver bangs hard, pulls yarns tight; sides go in. Thoughts, left lying around, get woven in.

But if you align yourself just as you do the loom—then in the clearness, you can hear the Song.

---

*In the Hopi culture, the men weave.

Sometimes Anglos Think It A Mistake In The Weaving.

It occurs in bordered rugs: the weaver makes a small, contrasting line from background through border to selvage. By its placement, the line penetrates the border and provides a Path through to the outside. I call it *The Weaver's Pathway*.

The need for a Pathway comes from the box-canyon fear of being enclosed on all sides with no way for escape. In a rug, the weaver fears that, in channeling all her energies and mental resources into a rug with an enclosing border, she may encircle and thereby entrap her spirit, mind, energies and design. Her future weaving work is in jeopardy. She must be able to use this design again successfully. Also at risk are her weaving muscles and vision. By vision is understood the ability to see, and also the ability to perceive designs—keep them in the head during weaving. This ability is sometimes equated with "sanity."

But, the Pathway is phasing out from disuse. In the 1930s it was recorded that roughly seven out of eight rugs contained the line. In 1970 my count of Pathways in bordered rugs totaled one out of eleven.*

Declining interest is reflected in the way weavers talk about the Pathway:

"I do it all the time."

"Mother did it. I don't put it in though; I just weave."

"That's old fashioned and I don't believe in it."

"You don't have to put it in each time—just whenever you remember."

Helen Tsinnie is a traditional weaver, with a special understanding of how weaving fits into the larger context of Life. She describes her method of making a Pathway:

> You put the gate [path] in at the top just before you're finished [closing the border]. You use the same color as your background is and you put it through to the outside, then back, then through to the outside, and then back in again. That way it makes four rows.
>
> We Navajos know that everything given to us in life was given to us in

*For additional data, see *The Weaver's Pathway*, Noël Bennett, 1974, Northland Press.

fours. We here on the reservation have four sacred mountains to protect us. There is one in the east, one in the south, one in the west and one in the north. There are four sacred colors: The east is white, the color of dawn. The south is blue, the color of the sky overhead at noon. The west is red, the color of the setting sun. And north is black, the color of night.

East, south, west and north. They go in the "sunwise" direction. Your inside direction is always facing east, just like the hogans. Just like the sun, you always start in the east and go sunwise. This sunwise is like you call clockwise.

Stones for jewelry were given to us in fours. We have white shell for the east and turquoise for south, coral and abalone shell for the west and jet for the north.

Earths for sandpainting, too. Medicinemen know where to get them—white, blue, red or black.

White is easy and for blue you can grind up turquoise. But if it's not available, then you can use greys, instead. Blues and greys are the same. For west, coral and browns are the same. Black is always black.

And of course you know that shell is for women. And turquoise is male. And coral is female, and black and night is always male. And if you keep on going with female and male each of the plants, each of the birds and animals is always male or female.

Then there's the corn and all the colors in the corn. Different ones are ground ceremonially depending on if the patient is male or female.

And for the weavers, our old-time sheep had four horns. The gods gave us the sheep in the four colors. They gave us the white sheep for the east, they gave us the grey sheep for the south, the brown sheep for the west and the black sheep for the north. And

even the brown sheep is called
dibéłchi'í—the red sheep.

Helen suggests that weaving a Pathway is
like asking for the reuse of design. Much
energy has gone into the weaving of the
blanket. If it's trapped within the border,
it can't get out for reuse.

When I put in the line, it's a time to
think-forward. I just say to myself:
"Thank you for letting me use this
design and I'd like to use it again
sometime."

Or other times I say, "Here's to the
next rug, may it be even better."

Illness Is Being Out-Of-Balance With The Universe.

The first step in healing is to consult someone who can divine which particular taboo has been broken. The Seer, the Hand Trembler, the Star Gazer. For instance, if the problem is an eye ailment, perhaps long ago as a child the patient opened the puppy's eyes before they were ready. Or perhaps while pregnant, the patient unintentionally looked at a dead animal along the road.

Once the cause of imbalance is determined, the patient consults the herbalist. With his knowledge of herbs and minerals, he concocts the potion which will alleviate the symptoms.

But the original transgression is yet to be righted, and the patient must still be brought into realignment with the Universe. It is the Singer who oversees this process. In his memory are chants and the complex perfection of designs known as sandpaintings.

Great dedication is required to become a Singer. Some nine-day ceremonies require different sandpaintings *each day*. Some singers know many different ceremonies. And

always, chants and designs cannot be recorded—only held in memory.

A Singer may work for an entire day painstakingly "drawing" intricate ceremonial figures on the hogan floor with grains of colored sand. When at dusk the "painting" is complete, the patient is brought in and seated upon the design. Amidst ceremonial chanting, universal sources of healing are called forth. Then, using a weaving batten, the Singer begins wiping clean the just-completed sandpainting. Never should healing power be drawn disproportionate to need. Never should the completed sandpainting be allowed to stand, dissipating its healing power.

And the Public Health Service doctor on reservation? He doesn't understand either origin of symptoms, or how to reunite a patient with the universe. But he is a superb symptom-reliever. So he's roughly equivalent to the herbalist.

The first time Jack and I were invited to a healing ceremony, I knew little of what to expect. I had been told that the ceremony would begin at dusk and end at dawn and

I had read that seating places in the hogan were traditional. The Medicineman-Singer is on the west side of the hogan; from this position he has a clear view through the east doorway and can thereby time chants according to moving star constellations. Assistants sit by him, the other men in the south, and the women around the north and east. All ceremonial actions are conducted in a "sunwise" direction—that is, clockwise around the central stove. I had been warned that there were lots of taboos that could be broken unintentionally by the unknowing novice (e.g. women are not to cross their legs), and that later, if the ceremony didn't work, people might blame it on the presence of an Anglo. I resolved not to do *anything* extraneous.

We arrived at dusk at the ceremonial hogan. A lot of people were already there. Was I late? My Navajo friend had just smiled and said, "Come when it's about dark." But nothing appeared to be happening; perhaps I was early. I stood uncertainly in the hogan doorway, specifically keeping my feet together and folding my arms as a silent reminder to slow down and not do anything out of self-consciousness.

I glanced inside the hogan. No other Anglos in attendance—none with whom to share the blame should something go wrong. Just as the book said, men were sitting in the west and south, women in the east and north. Though it was comforting to see both in their "right" places, the sheer numbers of people were disconcerting. Everyone was looking at me; everyone was sitting against the hogan wall. There was no vacant space for me, and no one indicated where I should sit either verbally or by making room. I was intent on not moving until I knew what to do, so I simply stood in the doorway silently repeating my mantra: "If you don't know what to do, do nothing." Finally, I noticed a space at my feet, just to the right of the door.

Trying to create as little disturbance as possible, I lowered myself slowly into the space. My bottom settled on the earthen floor and I felt relieved at becoming integrated with the group. But the Navajo lady to my right leaned toward me. "You have to go around the stove."

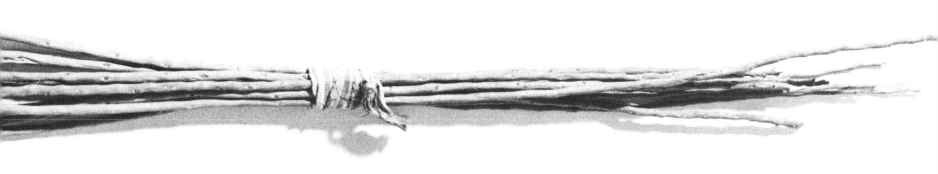

Sunwise! Clockwise! Even here in this little, two foot space? Fortunately, the cermony hasn't begun!

I stood back up and began the interminable journey around the center stove, front-stage center. I realized how difficult it was going to be to keep my wits. I hoped I was moving with dignity and that I hadn't disgraced the whole Anglo race with that unaware movement. Completing the circle, I gratefully slid back into the space I had vacated less than half a minute earlier.

"Dr. Bennett didn't take off his hat." It was the lady to my right again. I looked in the west. As a "professional courtesy," Jack had been invited to sit with the medicinemen. Not only had he been directed where to sit, but had been able to go to his place via a straight line. But, he now sat there with his improper hat. How could I signal him? I looked at him intensely, but our eyes never met. Suddenly, he simply reached up, removed his hat and placed it on a nail on the cedar log above him along with others. Inexplicably, the message had gotten through.

Soon, the patient was brought in, and by the light of the aromatic piñon fire the chanting began—an earthy, compelling unison of voices. The insistent stacatto drumbeat and male voice accent, periodically gave way to wailing falsetto. The room grew more intimate as the sound worked its way into crevice and pore. It seemed to connect to some primal part of me which hadn't been addressed before. I savored the unfamiliar sensation.

After a while I became engrossed with the Singers themselves. I had been told that chanting had to be continuous for the ceremony to be valid. I was concerned any irregularity might be blamed on my presence and I worried whenever the medicineman coughed or spat mid-song. But every time, an assistant's voice filled the void.

Chants lasted about a half-hour, followed by a short break during which people went in and out of the ceremonial hogan. Chill air flooded into my space beside the door everytime the door-blanket was pulled aside to admit someone. If I wanted to stretch my legs, or locate a juniper tree-bathroom, I would need to leave during a break and remain outside in the cold for a full song. I determined to stay inside all night—till dawn if need be.

My body relaxed. My breathing and heart slowed.

Keep a straight back for White Shell Woman.

I shifted positions, unaccustomed to sitting on the hard ground, careful not to cross my legs.

After a while, I felt drowsy, but nodding off was strictly forbidden. With effort I kept my eyes open to the end of the song. Then I relinquished my place, moving the two feet sunwise-to-the-left, and gratefully embraced the outside cold. The chill quickly cleared my head. I located the juniper tree. The walk stretched out my stiff muscles. I was back at the door of the hogan much before the ending of the chant, the only one outside. I tried jumping-jacks to keep off the chill while I plotted my reentry. Inside I'd noticed that new people coming in just walked clockwise to where they wished to sit. Wherever they stopped, people

moved aside to make room. I wanted a different spot directly in the north of the hogan, away from the breezy door. When a lull came in the chanting, I went back inside. This time no one leaned over to correct me.

Halfway through the night a different sort of break occured. The chanting stopped and the medicineman stood up and walked sunwise about the stove. He stood in front of the man sitting at the left of the hogan door and handed him something white. The seated man slowly untied a wrapping, revealing a pouch.

With index and thumb he removed a pinch of the contents and placed some on his tongue. He touched a second pinch to his forehead. A third time, he made a gesture as if to sprinkle about him, and handed the pouch to the man on his left. The new man made identical gestures. As did the next. Clearly the ritual would be coming full circle, and my turn would come.

Tongue, forehead, sprinkle.
As the pouch made its way around the circle, I suddenly remembered my grandmother's Catholic funeral. I was perhaps seven; it was was my first attendance of high mass. Latin chanting surrounded me. All of a sudden, unannounced, everyone stood up. Just as I stood up, everyone knelt. I too knelt, feeling the softness of the padded bench. The chanting continued and without warning, mid-word, everyone sat back in the pew. I didn't like being the only one out of sequence—The Incognizant. Sliding back slowly so no one would notice my belated sitting, thinking the sequence was stand/kneel/sit, I tightened my muscles. The next time I would be

ready to stand in unison.

At the first sense of movement I stood. Everyone else knelt. Again I was the lone pine on the prairie.

Tongue, forehead, sprinkle.
The corn pollen pouch was coming closer. Now it was midway—with the medicineman and his assistants. Fingers in the pouch, fingers to the tongue . . . I flashed back on the coughing and spitting of the singers all night. The incidence of tuberculosis among the Navajo was infamously high. Fingers from pouch to tongue to pouch. Was the substance in the pouch a good medium for transmittal? Perhaps I could just put it to my lips. Would anyone notice? Would this negate the pouch ritual? Would this negate the ceremony?

The pouch was being handed to the lady next to me. Her movements were precise, unhurried. My body identified with the gestures, knowing I would be next.

This might be my only ceremony ever. I have to do it right!
Even if I don't live out the age of thirty.
I recklessly gave myself to the hands of

fate and reached for the pouch.

> *Pouch in my right hand; give it to my*
> *left—the leather is soft and pliable.*
> *Right hand fingers into the pouch*
> *—the narrow opening softly encloses*
> *my thumb and forefinger.*
> *I withdraw a pinch.*
> *Fingers to the tongue*
> *—I taste the dry sweet granules of corn*
> *pollen.*
> *Fingers in, then to the forehead*
> *— ah, the last motion was for the body,*
> *this one for the mind.*
> *Fingers in, I sprinkle the pollen about*
> *me*
> *— I'm suddenly generous. I'm offering*
> *a prayer for everyone everywhere.*

I pause at the conclusion, echoing the
rhythm of those before me. I hand it to
the next lady. She won't take it.

> *Tongue. Forehead. Sprinkle. I did it*
> *right! I even put it on my tongue. She*
> *won't take it. I gave it to her in my right*
> *hand and she won't take it. I'll try my*
> *left.*

I offer it and she takes it. And in the space
between dusk and dawn I watch the
pouch complete its sunwise journey.

> *Sunwise. Sunwise. All ceremonial*
> *actions are sunwise! Facing the stove, I*
> *take the pouch in my right hand and*
> *give it with my left! It must come*
> *through me, sunwise.*

The next time I'm invited to a puberty rite
ceremony, I feel good about the
prospects. I have an idea of what to do
and what to expect. I dress in the satin
skirt and velvet blouse I've made for the
occasion. I know people will look at me
the whole time; I'm the only Anglo
woman present. I pull on my moccasins
with the old silver buttons. This time they
will have something beautiful to look at.

At dusk, at the ceremonial hogan, I
stand at the entrance. People are sitting all
over inside, perhaps three times the
number in the last ceremony. Besides
those around the periphery, the space
between them and the stove is also filled.
Jack sits just to the left of the door (once
again he is not required to go around the
stove). And I know that I just have to
head for a spot where I will stop and
people will make space.

Sunwise I set off around the stove and

halt in the north near the stove. A space appears and I sit. At first I'm grateful for the warmth, and then I realize I've probably selected the worst spot of all; it is too hot. It would be plenty warm around the perimeter of the hogan with so many people packed in. Also, if I were in back I'd be out of everyone's view. And I'd have the hogan wall to lean against, to keep my back straight.

I take time to look at everyone who is joining in ceremony on behalf of the patient. I do not recognize many faces. I note that Jack has removed his hat. There is a closeness of body odors from many people together in a confined space. I will not be able to shift positions without bumping people right, left and back. I relax to avoid cramping muscles. The chanting begins. I navigate a break with relative ease and return to a new position during the next song lull. I feel much more at home at my second ceremony.

Now it is time for the passing of the corn pollen pouch. There is a growing murmur of Navajo words among medicineman and assistants. They look at the first person next to the door where

the pouch must begin. It is Jack. Does the Anglo know what to do? Should we give him the pouch? It must start there!

The medicineman rises, walks clockwise about the stove, and silently extends the pouch. Jack unhurriedly unwinds the wrapping, and slowly reaches in to place the pollen on his tongue, then in again to place it on his forehead, and then in for the sprinkle. Slowly he passes it with his left hand to the person to his left. I feel the tension leave.

And here it is, zig-zagging its way around the circle. It looks familiar, like an old friend, and I watch it wind its way from the back to the front of the hogan in its sunwise journey. My turn comes and I reach for it with my right hand, give it to my left. I wait for the prescribed second. I'm taking enough time, not rushing the process, staying in touch with the meaning. I extrapolate: the tongue internalizes the thought, forehead is akin to psyche, the sprinkle universalizes the action. The sequence feels like an inter- nalized gesture. The pouch is in my left hand, ready to hand to the lady on my left. I realize that the lady behind me to my right hasn't yet had a turn. I reach across and hand it to her; she won't take it.

Last time, the lady was on my left and she took it from my left hand. Now that she's on my right, maybe I use my right. I change hands and offer it. She still won't take it. I am struggling to stay calm and clear.

I offered it to her in my left hand and she wouldn't take it. I offered it to her in my right. Wouldn't take it. It must be the left. It's got to be the left! Last time it was the left. I put it in my left hand and do the only thing I can think of. Turn and reach around behind me to offer her the sacred pouch. She takes it. And the pouch completes its circle.

Sunwise. Sunwise. Right hand brings it in, left sends it forth. The pouch comes through me. When I cross my arm over, the pouch doesn't go through me; I close myself to the circle; the lady doesn't take it. But, by reaching around behind me, the pouch goes through me. And I am open to the circle.

Lessons from passing the pouch:

Learning visually with no feedback is difficult.

Previous learnings may not hold up in new situations.

The answer is always inherent in the question, the solution in the problem . . . but I must be unrushed and trusting to find it.

Anglo Medicine Wasn't Enough. "Perhaps A Ceremony . . . "

Jack had "cured" a man of a serious illness. All symptoms were gone, but something more was needed. A ceremony?

The patient agreed, and when arrangements were made, he invited the doctor's family.

Like other ceremonies, chanting began at dusk inside the hogan and would continue to dawn. Halfway through the night, however, the chanting stopped, the medicineman got up, began talking amiably in Navajo with the people around him, and walked outside. Everyone followed. So we did, too. Outside, people were preparing food. Soon people sat— some together, some scattered—with plates of fry-bread and mutton stew. We stood away from the group, leaning against our jeep, watching and waiting for someone to invite us to join in. Nobody motioned us closer nor even particularly noticed us. Six-year-old Shawn spotted the fry-bread. Could I get him some? I assured him he could have some when the time was right, but we didn't want to intrude; we were waiting to be invited.

Fifteen minutes later, *status quo* unchanged, I asked Jack the obvious. "You're sure we're invited?" He nodded an unequivocal reply.

Perhaps no one was offering us food because no one knew we liked it. Many PHS doctors and wives had privately confided they hated the taste of mutton and were repelled by the lack of sanitation in preparation. This new family, to whom we were strangers, had no way of knowing we ate anything cooked.*

Everyone around us continued eating, and Shawn grew more impatient. Couldn't I just go get him a piece of fry-bread? I suggested that we go home, instead. Eat, and return.

Jack considered my idea. "You know, we've been to a lot of these things. And everytime something goes wrong, we always tell ourselves afterwards we should have just hung in quietly. Maybe we

---

*We had been warned not to drink the local water. This caution had further been impressed by the experience of a physician friend who had hiked into a remote area and drank from a local well. He was six months recovering from hepatitis.

should stay a while and see what happens."

"I know. But it sure is difficult." I sat on the ground to wait it out.

Ten minutes later Jack was reconsidering. "You really think we ought to go home and eat?"

"By now, it's too late—we'll miss the ceremony." I nodded toward increasing activity around the ceremonial hogan. People were already starting to clean up. A few were going back into the hogan—the medicineman among them.

"You mean we're never going to get any fry-bread?" Shawn wailed.

I continued offering alternatives. Perhaps we should just go into the hogan with everyone else and forget the idea of food. Or maybe just go home and go to bed: after all, it was 3 o'clock in the morning, and Jack had to work the next day. We had at least experienced half a healing ceremony.

Just as sleep was sounding better all the time, a large flash of movement distracted us from our discussion. A line of women, seven abreast, headed toward us. Each woman carried a large container of food. One had a pan of mutton stew, one a pot of coffee, one a whole watermelon, another a large stack of fry bread. Two others carried a galvanized tub with soft drink cans on ice. I looked behind us to see where they were heading. Nobody was back there. They set the food down before us, said something in Navajo and left. All that food must be for us.

So much delicious food! Much more than we could possibly eat. The chanting began inside the hogan. We leisurely enjoyed our meal. At a lull in the song, we joined others inside. Our stomachs were full and our faith restored.

Days later, I was still wondering about the food. Why had the women changed their mind and brought it to us after all? Unable to unravel the riddle alone, I went to visit Tiana Bighorse. I sat with her and watched her weave for a couple hours. Then I told the story.

"We waited a long time," I summarized. "Almost everyone else had gone back into the hogan. Jack knew we had been invited, but we worried we weren't really welcome.''

My friend continued flicking wefts through narrow warp spaces, then beat them in place with the fork. The rhythm, set by fifty years of refining, was unerring. I had told my story. I had not directly asked for an explanation, but I was preserving the silence in which one could be given.

Her small body commanded the towering loom like the organist at the Mormon Tabernacle . . . effortlessly coordinating each shimmering strand . . . manipulating and strumming vertical warps forward and back to create openings . . . slicing colors through patterns to interweave a symphonic complexity of visual tones. She never missed a note or beat. But in time the rhythm slowed, then stopped. With fork hand resting in her lap, the symphonist looked at me quizzically.

"Don't you know?" There was a nasal tone of disbelief in her voice. "The guest is *always* served last.''

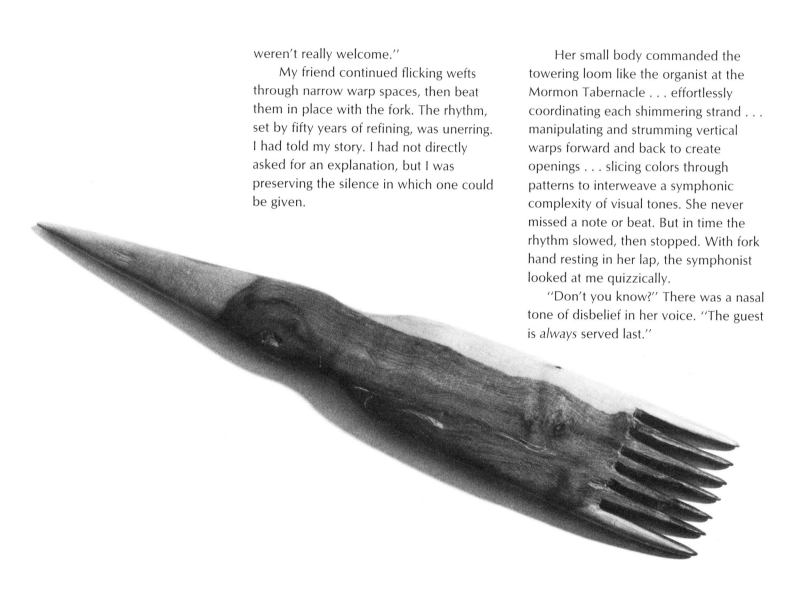

"I Can't Believe That Somewhere In The World There Is Water As Far As The Eye Can See."

Tiana and I were sitting at her loom. We had been talking about White Shell Woman, who is considered a role model for women generally, and a special benefactress for weavers. I was telling Tiana I had heard that White Shell Woman originated near the Catalina Islands off the California coast. From there, we had gotten on the subject of the ocean. I tried to imagine how immense, powerful and foreign the ocean would seem to someone who had always lived in the desert.

I remembered an incident a year before. Tiana and I were driving together to Flagstaff. She was reaching into her purse on the floor. As if frozen in motion, she held the position. Then, at some specific moment, she slowly withdrew her hand and rested it on the scantly open window beside her. When she returned her hand to her lap, there seemed a sense of completion.

I wondered what she was doing. A slip of white leather was visible in her open purse—the tip of a corn pollen pouch? Maybe she had put a pinch of pollen out the window. If so, why then? The rear view mirror reflected the receding image of a bridge sign. We had just crossed the Little Colorado River.

I didn't want to invade her privacy, so I didn't ask. Several miles down the road, she answered anyway.

"So there will always be enough water for everyone."

Now, sitting at her loom, and remembering how significant a small amount of water had been to her, I thought about how she would feel seeing the vast, rolling ocean. I couldn't pay the cost of getting her there, but somehow I'd find a way.

"I'll call some weaving guilds and see if any would like a presentation on Navajo weaving," my mother brain-stormed that evening on the phone in California. "You could pay for your trip; she can demonstrate and you can talk. You can stay with us." The idea seemed workable to me, but I wondered how Tiana would feel.

Here was a traditional Navajo woman of fifty-eight, who had scarcely been off-reservation. Would going to the big city be scary? And she was used to the solitude and silence of the vast Southwest. How could she demonstrate for a crowd? A crowd of Anglos asking questions.

When I saw her next, I told her Mom's idea and filled in the unknowns the best I could. I thought we could arrange the demonstrations in a month. That was O.K. with her. We would drive to the Grand Canyon airport and fly from there to San Francisco. My mother would meet us at the airport.

"O.K."

It seemed I was the only one worried.

On the planned day, I picked her up at the hogan. She wore a newly made satin skirt; a plum, plush velvet blouse; turquoise rings, bracelets and necklaces. Her extra clothes were neatly rolled in a dark blue-and-rust-fringed Pendleton blanket. I put them next to my suitcase. On our way to the Grand Canyon airport, a deer crossed the road. "A sign of good luck," she said. I was relieved it hadn't been an owl.*

The airplane's engines revved and we were soon airborne. Right after takeoff, the stewardess came over to make her feel welcome.

"Is this your first flight? Yes? Well we hope you enjoy it and are comfortable. Where are you from? You must be Indian with that beautiful turquoise. What is your name?"

I cringed. As none of the answers had come fast enough for the stewardess, she reached for the airline tickets to get her answer. "Tiana Bighorse. Well, Tiana, we certainly are glad to have you aboard. Do you know how high we are flying today?" The questions rolled one after the other, leaving no time for a thoughtful reply. And the familiar first name** was punctuating alternate sentences.

"Twenty-five thousand feet!" The

---

*An owl is a sign of bad luck. Its appearance sometimes foretells witchery or even death.

**One's name is a personal possession, spoken aloud with least possible frequency. When its usage is unavoidable, as when interfacing with Anglos at the PHS hospital, the more formal Mr. or Mrs. with the surname only, is considered least objectionable.

stewardess immediately answered her own question. The quantifying high number meant nothing to Tiana so she said nothing. Her silence, however, did not impede the stewardess who was well-trained in putting passengers at ease. "Tiana, do you know how fast we are going? No? Six hundred miles an hour!"

A smile of amazement broke across my friend's face. "Oh! And I tell my son, Leonard, he's driving too fast when he goes sixty!"

The stewardess laughed. I was amazed at how well Tiana was handling the onslaught. This was just the kind of situation that had been concerning me. She was entering a foreign culture. I had meant to prepare her.

After the stewardess left, I began slowly. "There's a few things I want to tell you about the trip and California." Tiana turned her head to listen. "In California, people are friendly. And they like to show you they are friendly, and so they call you by your first name. Even if they don't know you." She nodded, and said nothing.

"The second thing is that these people are going to ask lots of questions—I mean *lots* of questions! Even more than I used to ask when I first came to the reservation. Most Anglos don't know how to learn by watching, so they ask even when the answer is in front of them." She nodded.

I had talked enough for the moment. Now I would be quiet and wait. I reclined my seat and looked out the window. I still needed to prepare her for eye contact. In the Navajo way, looking into someone's eyes is disrespectful. It's also a method used in witching. When I first came to the reservation, I had a hard time learning to look away, at jewelry, hands, feet— anything but the eyes. Now I could imagine how uncomfortable it could be for my friend, surrounded by intense, friendly Californians, all trained from birth in direct eye contact.

"You know, you don't have to tell me this," her quiet words broke into my thoughts. "Sallie already told me," she explained simply.

"What did Sallie tell you?"

"Sallie said, 'Mom, now look. You're going to California. And for goodness

sake, look right at people's eyes when they talk to you. Otherwise they're going to think that you're shifty and irresponsible. And that you just stole something!' ''

Once in California, the presentations went well. Tiana answered questions quickly and clearly, looking directly at each person and selecting basic words she knew. On several occasions she told people she was grateful for the chance to come to California to demonstrate the weaving she loved. She was pleased at their interest, the young girls especially. I was amazed at her newly acquired cross-cultural skills.

Then came our free day, the one to fulfill the purpose of the trip. We drove to Point Lobos for her first magnificent view of the ocean. At the water's edge, she put her hand into her purse.

''Which way is South?''

I pointed one way; Mom pointed forty-five degrees in another direction. We looked at each other and laughed.

We were at a complicated section of coastline, with promontories and bays at every view. It was difficult to determine south. I carefully explained all this, but even as the words were being formed I knew that something was wrong. Tiana's question had nothing to do with a map. It had to do with her being Navajo, and always knowing where she was in relation to the four cardinal points.

The fact that she was even asking confirmed what I already knew. She was disoriented. For Mom and I not to agree on south, was to us an amusing difference of opinion. And entirely different from Tiana not *knowing* which way was South.

Each of the past four mornings she had awakened with the question: "Which way is East?"

I had opened the curtains of our bedroom window to show her the sun mounting the city buildings outside. Each morning she said she could see that, but it didn't *feel* like East. Then I would talk about how flying often scrambles directions. Next time driving might be better. Or maybe after she was here

awhile, the directions might straighten themselves out.

Now she was asking about South. Short of a compass, there was no way to be sure. The sun was directly overhead; Mom knew the area better than I; her sense of direction had always been good. We picked a point closer to Mom's finger and agreed. Out came the corn pollen pouch and a liberal sprinkling. I joined in the blessing, remembering her words of the year before: "So there will always be enough water for all."

At the end of the trip we drove from the Grand Canyon back to Tuba City and the hogan. All the way I talked about California. It had been an exciting week. My parents had enjoyed being with her. We had paid our way and learned a lot, besides. Tiana agreed. And the next week arranged for a Blessing Way Ceremony to reorient her to the four sacred directions.

Tádídíín—
Corn Pollen—A Word As Light As The Substance Itself.

Tádídíín—used as a prayer when gathering dye plants and again when greeting the dawn. The more I learned about it, the more I wished one day to have a corn pollen pouch of my own.

I first wondered aloud to Tiana Bighorse if it would be all right for me as an Anglo to have a pouch. After some time she replied, "You just have to make it. I think it's okay."

I was exhilarated. Yet, how to begin? I recalled that the pouch must be made only of "unwounded deer skin." How could I get such a piece?

"In the old days, three ways. In those days hunters were fast and strong. They could run with the deer, wrestle it, break its neck. They could suffocate it with corn-pollen. They could run it off the cliff."

"And now?"

"Nowdays, when a deer has been hit by a car, it's okay. Just not shot."

To my knowledge there were no deer in the Tuba City area of the reservation.

Occasionally as our family drove at night to the Grand Canyon, I saw the staring, light-entranced eyes; yet a constant vigil of the side of the road yielded nothing. Months passed—October, November and then it was December, time for Christmas in California.

We met my parents mid-way. Since there were two cars, my father, husband and son teamed to drive one, while Mom and I drove the other. She and I decided on a more scenic back route.

Driving along, mile after mile, mesmerized by the warmth of the day and endless green California foliage, I was startled by a large dead animal by the side of the road. Slowly I pulled the car onto the shoulder and explained to my mother. We had just passed a dead deer and I needed a piece of skin for a ceremonial pouch. Was there a knife in the car? A complete search yielded nothing, but my mother saw we were near a farmhouse. Maybe we could borrow one there.

At the old house, I rapped on the weathered door. No answer. I knocked harder. Then I heard a shuffling of steps.

The door opened a scant two inches and eyes peered suspiciously through the crack.

"What do you want?" The voice was a raspy whisper.

"Do you have a knife we could borrow?" I looked away, trying to think of a plausible reason why we would want to borrow a knife out here in the middle of nowhere. But when I glanced back the door was tightly shut.

Several minutes later it reopened, again a crack, and a butcher cleaver was passed through handle first. I thanked the unseen-one, promised to return it right away, and hastily headed down the road.

When I had spoken to Tiana Bighorse earlier, it had not occurred to me to ask how to go about this delicate task—nor had I thought to ask from which part of the deer I should cut. I regretted for the first time that my high school biology teacher had not required the dissection of a frog—as had my older sister's. Why, I had never dissected anything! There's always the first time, I reminded myself. After all, the deer is already dead.

The deadness of the deer became poignantly clearer as we rounded the corner. A breeze blowing from the direction of the bulky, stiffened form told us the animal was past its prime for skin-taking. With disappointment, and perhaps greater relief, we returned to the car and then to the ranch house. There I passed the unused knife back through the crack. And there was no sound as the door shut once more.

Eight months later a small square special-delivery package came in the mail. When I opened one corner, a profusion of salt scattered about. Expecting food of some sort, I continued unfolding the soft multi-layered paper until nestled at the core I found a brown, crusty, salt-caked rectangle. Close examination revealed a fur-side, and I recognized the most valued present I could hope to receive: a 5"x 6" piece of coveted deerskin. The box had been addressed by my mother. Yet, *she* hadn't skinned the deer; of that I was sure. I wondered who my benefactor might be.

Over the phone my mother explained that our Christmastime-deer-incident had remained in her thoughts. So months later while driving to work, when she saw a dead deer by the side of the road, she noted its location, planning to ask my brother to "lift" a piece of skin later in the evening. But by evening, it was gone; the efficient California State Highway Department had neatly cleared the roadside of all "clutter." The following week there was yet another deer. At home she looked for my brother, but he was nowhere to be found. When at the end of a full day of extractions, my dentist-father came in tired and inquired routinely if there was anything he might do before sitting a moment, the solution seemed to present itself.

So by dim light and employing dental tools, my dad had gently and professionally removed a piece of deerskin for his daughter.

By the time the package had arrived via mail, we were living in Shonto, and so several weeks passed before Shawn and I were able to drive back to Tuba City to talk again with Tiana Bighorse, and learn the next step in The-Making-Of-A-Pouch.

After several hours, when the conversation was free to take its course, I eased into the subject. What, I asked, would a person do once they had some buckskin? Tiana immediately asked how I had gotten a piece. While I told her the story, she examined the crusty remnant. What was all the salt for? You don't need that! And the piece was a bit small, but maybe it would do. And what part of the deer had my father taken it from? The belly? That was okay. The next step would be tanning.

I had already had several experiences of trying to tan a sheepskin to sit on while weaving. Each new method had yielded varying degrees of non-success. So when my friend began to describe the process involved, I listened carefully. I knew the job ahead would not be easy. When the time came, I would be grateful for every word she was now offering.

First, I would be using baked sheep-brains; their oil makes the skin soft and pliable. To prepare them I should singe a sheep-head over open fire, then bury it in the ground and continue to burn the fire above. After the baking, about two to three hours depending on the size of the fire, I would remove the brains and start the tanning.

That evening, back home around the dinner table, I proposed buying another sheep for the freezer. The family agreed and the next day I made the necessary arrangements. As I had already gone through similar negotiations once before, I knew what to expect when I spoke with this Navajo neighbor.

Did I want him to kill the sheep for us?

"Yes."

Did I want the fleece?

"Yes."

He looked a bit surprised at the answer, but continued

How about the head?

"Yes."

His eyes showed disbelief. The intestines, then. Them too?

"No, you can have them."

He smiled in a sort of pleased, sort of puzzled way and agreed. A few weeks later he reappeared with a sheep: meat, fleece and head.

Our Public Health Service housing, where we were required to live, was furnace-heated. No fireplace, no woodpile. Now I had a sheep head and was laying plans to bake it. I needed to gather wood. It took Shawn and me one full day to scout the area, locate almost non-existent trees, and fill the back of our jeep with dry branches.

The following morning I readied myself for fire-building. The wind was strong and gusty and I wished for my eagle-scout brother. Obviously Tiana had neglected to tell me a windless day would be best. Probably assumed I knew that much. With perseverance I coaxed a flame and then, afraid it would go out, piled the wood high. The smoke billowed profusely. Finally the wood caught and blazed, and in a few hours I had coals.

I steadied an old grate and put on the sheep head. As flames licked the eyelashes, I suddenly began to question the whole process. Why was it necessary to singe anyway? And how much should I singe? Of course, nobody was there to advise me. So at some indeterminate time I pronounced it "done," removed head and coals, buried it as I'd been directed,

and then busied myself with keeping the fire going.

And how much fuel it burned!! Frequently I worried that the once-immense cedar pile would run out and I would have to leave in the middle of "baking" to get more. But the wind soon died down and fire-tending settled into a pleasant, hypnotic state.

One hour. Two hours. She had said two to three. There was still a bit of wood. Better to cook it well. I didn't want to have to repeat the whole process again. Then, at exactly two-and-a-half-hours-and-unable-to-wait-any-longer, I extinguished the fire. But as I removed dirt and coals, I became mindful of a growing queasiness. How would a singed, baked sheep head look?

Just as my shovel struck buried head, Shawn woke from his afternoon nap and called out from inside the house. I was grateful for the interruption and went into his bedroom. I told him he'd awakened just in time to help me dig up the head; together we could finish the job. He was excited to be included.

As soon as I stepped back into the bright sunlight, I knew something was wrong. The hole was already dug. Even more alarming, it was empty! Shawn saw the crisis at the same moment and was instantly wide awake. He rushed into action, charging around the corner of the house, yelling with authority, "Blaze, NO!"

Our well-trained dog, who never begged for food while we were eating, and who wouldn't think of taking delicacies off an unguarded picnic table, had found the Aroma-of-Baked-Sheep-Head irresistable.

I retrieved the head—never even faltered at how it looked. I was so relieved at not losing it altogether.

The task now was how best to get at the brains. When I had asked Tiana Bighorse how to remove them from the head, she had told me to use an ax. Then perhaps seeing my uncertainty, she had added that they would be toward the back of the head, and once the head was open they could be spooned out.

Now, surveying the singed head before me, ax in hand, I explained the intent to Shawn who was watching the whole process matter-of-factly.

"Now all we have to do is to open the head and remove the brains." But I had other worries. How hard should I strike it? What if when I hit, the head wouldn't open? How many times would I have to hit it? On the other hand, what if the first time I hit it, I smashed it altogether— brains included? At this fortuitous moment my husband came home from his day at the clinic.

After listening to my concerns, Jack, the anatomist, the surgeon, calmly reconsidered available tools, decided on a hack-saw, and deftly lopped off a portion of the skull precisely in the right area. With some pride he informed me we were encountering the occipital pole, and continued in his informative manner to point out the various anatomical landmarks. For my part, however, I was hearing little—happy just to have the brains in a container. As I cleaned up for the evening, I was very well satisfied. After years of struggling and skimping, medical school had finally, and most unexpectedly, paid off.

The next morning I leapt from bed to the project-in-progress. Today would be the day to actually tan that piece of hide my father had cut for me over a year ago. When all was quiet, I carefully got out the "recipe cards." They began:

TANNING PROCEDURES
First, soak the hide in water, soften it and remove the hair.

This seemed simple enough and I began with confidence. It took but a few moments to discover the obstacles. To remove the hair, the knife had to be very sharp; to shave it close, I had to scrape the skin. There seemed a real danger that in the process the skin itself might be cut. But in spite of my concerns the work went well and I finished three hours later, pleased with the results.

Dilute the brains with water and rub them well into the hide.
Directions for working the skin followed.

From my past tanning of sheep skins I expected this would be the most difficult and important part. Always before, the finished hides were too stiff, scarcely pliable. Our Navajo friends all told us that though Shawn and I had rubbed and massaged the hide until our knuckles were sore and our fingers aching, we had stopped too soon. Someone explained that for a real good job, four men would take turns rubbing in the brains.

Tanning also seemed to be regarded as somewhat of a ceremonial ordeal. It was considered bad luck to eat at any time during the process. There should be no interruptions—the rubbing, stretching, working of the hide must be continuous. Fortunately, this piece of buckskin was small—a mere five by six inches. I could see it would take days to tan the whole animal well, going it alone.

I closed the window curtains to provide privacy and reached for the brains and deerskin. But just then the door-bell rang. Reluctantly I washed my hands, and shut the kitchen door where the drama had been about to begin.

At the front door stood a Navajo friend about my age and her mother, who spoke no English. They had come to see the "Doctor's-Wife-Who-Weaves." Under other circumstances I would have been glad for the visit. Even now I considered their coming an honor. Certainly, I told myself, I had not actually begun the rubbing. Therefore, this could not be considered an interruption.

I knew they wanted to see me weave—all visitors did. No one believed an Anglo could actually do it. I usually enjoyed demonstrating, sitting, talking, exchanging dye recipes. But today my mind was on the deerskin and I was concerned about what would happen if much time went by. Or if it were discovered.

The daughter settled into a chair, making herself comfortable for a visit; but the mother stood by the door. They were now speaking intently in Navajo. The daughter translated:

"My mother says she smells sheep-brains."

I reluctantly admitted she was right—that I was about to tan a piece of deerskin for a corn-pollen pouch.

The mother strode past me through the kitchen door.

"It's a good thing we came," she announced through her daughter. "I know just what to do. And if you make it wrong, it sure is bad luck. I'll sit here while you do it right. You have to finish it all at one time. And don't eat in the middle!"

And so began a long afternoon of kneading, rubbing, stretching, massaging. When at dusk my hands ached and the piece was done and dry, I caressed the white skin against my cheek. It was unbelievably soft.

Tiana had said the piece was "somewhat small" and that I should stretch it out as much as I could in the tanning. Now that I had done this, I wondered if it was big enough for a pouch. Tiana was also concerned about something else. The actual corn pollen pouch had to be made by a medicineman. She had asked around and found a medicineman who "would do it for an Anglo." But, she explained, it couldn't be done at just any time; the making of the pouch had to correspond with a Hózhǫ́ǫ́jí, a "Blessing Way" Ceremony. The medicineman she had spoken to had no Hózhǫ́ǫ́jí planned right away, so there was nothing to do but wait.

Months passed. Whenever I passed by the skin, I marveled in the suede-side softness, the smooth-side pureness. I often wondered about its future. One day another weaver came for a visit. As we were talking, I remembered that her husband was a medicineman and he performed the Hózhǫ́ǫ́jí. Impulsively I confided my story. I told her how I had gotten the unwounded deer skin and that recently I had tanned it with sheep brains. Now I was wondering how it would ever be made into a pouch. She asked to see it.

She looked it over carefully, said it was well tanned and that she thought it big enough. Almost as an aside she added that there was a Hózhǫ́ǫ́jí that weekend, and, saying nothing more, pocketed my piece and left. It happened so fast! Before I knew it the piece was gone. I watched her back disappearing down the road.

All week, all week-end, I worried. The skin was so small, so easily lost. Perhaps I should have waited and given it to the medicineman Tiana Bighorse knew. Perhaps in my eagerness, I had acted too hastily in turning it over to this weaver's husband whom I had scarcely met. Monday morning I stayed home, certain she would bring it at any moment, but by afternoon there was still no sign of her. I considered going to her house but didn't want to seem untrusting. I managed to wait until the following day.

The next morning, when I got to her house, I was relieved just to find her there. She invited me in and we talked generally. An hour passed without mention of the pouch. Finally I brought up the ceremony.

Yes, there had been a Hózhǫ́ǫ́jí over the weekend.

Silence.

Had she spoken with her husband about the pouch? Was he willing to make it?

Silence.

"Yes."

Silence.

I tried one last question, afraid I was asking too much. But I was desperate for reassurance.

"When could I see it?"

Again silence, and then, "In a few days."

I didn't understand what was going on. Had he lost the leather and had to replace it? No, probably he had the leather but had decided not to make it for an Anglo after all, and my friend didn't know how to tell me. I was weighing other possibilities when she began to explain.

The pouch was made at the ceremony but it had to stay in the same hogan for four days to receive full blessing: a day for the east, a day for the south, a day for the west and a day for the north. I nodded. I still didn't know what was going on. I returned to the subject of weaving, which I did understand, and soon after went home, leaving the pouch to fate.

It was many days after A-Day-For-The-North when the medicineman and his wife knocked on my door. At first I didn't recognize him. He had a black, curly Halloween wig plopped on his head. Maybe he had been drinking. But no, he had no smell of alcohol and he talked perfect sense. Something was going on. I don't know what. Probably never will.

I invited them in, the wig came off, the conversation began with family, then turned to weaving. Then casually out of the medicineman's jacket pocket—safe and well-cared for—came a beautifully transformed pouch.

It was white and slender—wide at the bottom easing to a narrow neck where it was tied with a matching thong. My fingers traced crevice and contour. I thought of how long it had taken me to get the hide, the traumatic baking of the sheep head, my swollen knuckles during tanning. And now there were the unknown miracles of its creation. I held the whole of it, and in that moment understood the preciousness of each ceremonial item.

It takes the maker's Spirit—time, knowledge, energy and will—to bring a ceremonial item into being. So, the power it draws on is great.

And when the medicineman told me I would need to gather corn pollen now for my pouch, I readied myself. I knew, even before hearing, that the process would not be easy. That in my very slow journey of knowing, pollen collecting would be just one small step.

And one more thing. This step would not be the last.

The ceremony for weaving is a "Blessing Way."
A renewal-way.
A communal-way.
Clan and kinsmen bring food.
Medicinemen invoke the Good.

With the white, the yellow corn is ground.
The colors of corn for women.
And all the weaving tools immersed.
To nourish.
To replenish.

The song that is sung
has a phrase that's repeated:
T'áá áhót'é
"Nothing will lessen or leave."

A promise of wealth.
A promise of worth.

T'áá áhót'é
"Nothing will lessen or leave."

Fair-Haired Richard Had A Way About Him—

a respect toward Life generally—a certain New England reserve. Perhaps that was why he had been permitted to live in the Zuni Village—an honor not often allowed an Anglo. He was teaching English in the Zuni schools and learning weaving from me at the University of New Mexico in Gallup. He was also studying with the potter, Daisy Hooee. Daisy was a granddaughter of the famous Hopi potter, Nampeyo, but she had married a Zuni man and was living at the Zuni pueblo.

During the preceding year, Daisy had been bitten seriously by a snake and had gone to the Public Health Service Hospital. But the doctors were unable to help her. Then she went to the Zuni medicineman and was healed. Because of the miracle, Daisy was given the honor of extending her home openly as one of the Shalako* homes. Daisy had personally asked Richard to come to her home for the event, and he had accepted.

One evening, Richard was sitting at home reading. Suddenly, the door opened and a line of Zuni elders walked in and stood around the table at which

Richard was sitting. For a moment, Richard thought they might be there to tell him to leave—so few Anglos had been permitted to stay. He didn't know what to do. But, he remembered what I had learned from the Navajo: "If you don't know what to do, do nothing."

So he stood up and looked down, feet together, arms folded. No one spoke or moved.

Just then he remembered Shalako. There was always a lot of food at the ceremony. Maybe the food came from the village generally. Maybe the elders were here for food on behalf of Shalako. He wasn't sure, but it seemed he couldn't go wrong making an offering. Silently he went to his small pantry.

What does one offer the revered Shalako?

He scanned the shelves of canned clams and cranberry sauce. Certainly New England fare. He would have liked to offer corn he had grown in the earth itself, ground by hand into meal and

---

*a winter ceremony involving twelve-foot-tall masked personages called Shalako.

transformed into traditional food. But there was none on the shelves.

How much food do you give Shalako?

Better to give too much than too little. Richard brought everything from his pantry to the table, stepped back, folded his arms, looked down at the mud floor.

Maybe I haven't given enough. Maybe the foods I have given are an insult. But he had no more to give, so he looked up. The elders had disappeared. So had the food.

What had happened? He sat down, stunned. Tried to sort things out. Picked up his book, but couldn't concentrate. Finally, Richard went to bed for a sleepless night.

The next day at his regular pottery lesson, Daisy said to him, "I heard the elders visited your home last evening."

He nodded.

"The elders were pleased you knew to give them food." Richard dipped his brush and continued painting his pot. "And that you knew to say a silent prayer before and after offering it.

"But what pleased them most was that you knew not to look at them while they were taking it."

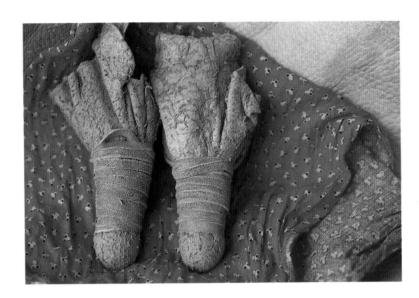

T'áá áhót'éhí
T'áá áhót'éhí

Traveling Alone The Visible Path Can Lead To Criticism And, Sometimes, Witchery.

In 1970 I thought about making a book on Navajo weaving to use in Navajo boarding schools and at Navajo Community College. The craft was dying out. Young Navajo girls had no place to learn.

I also thought Anglo weavers could benefit from knowing Navajo weaving methodology and philosophy. I asked Tiana Bighorse if she would like to co-author the book. I told her she should think about it and talk it over with her family. The next time we were together, she told me she had decided to do it.

But I wanted her to be sure. So, several months later I asked her again. Again, she said "yes." The third time was the same. The fourth time, she brought an end to my asking,

"You ask me lots of times; I already say 'yes.' "

Ten years later I was coordinating a national conference on Navajo weaving. Three hundred collectors, dealers, researchers, restorers would come together in Santa Fe for three intense days

of learning. Thirty experts would share their knowledge on the history, dyes, wools and dating of Navajo textiles. I called the conference "Shared Horizons."

Of course, these people must see the weaving process in action. So, I wrote Tiana and asked if she would demonstrate. When she wrote back, I understood the courage that allowed her to say "Yes."

Whenever I was at a ceremony on the reservation, it felt good to have a familiar face close by. Being alone with strangers speaking another language was unsettling. I didn't want my friend to experience that. Now, I would be busy making the conference run smoothly, so I asked my mother to be with Tiana, interpret what was going on, generally attend to her comfort. I also suggested that Sallie and Paul come with her. The conference would pay their way, too.

The second evening of the conference I asked Tiana how things were going, demonstrating.

"Fine. But you haven't been there."

"Yes. I've been busy with the conference. But, maybe I could miss a

lecture tomorrow morning. We could
have breakfast together. It would be just
an hour. I wish it were longer and that I
didn't have a time limit.'' She said she
understood.

Over her order of coffee, pancakes
and bacon, she told me the story of her
coming to Santa Fe.

"You know, I've been sick. Two
months ago, I think maybe I'm not
coming. I just wake up one morning and
I'm dizzy. And the room is turning around
and I'm throwing up. And I just keep
throwing up. And Sallie say, 'Mom, we
better take you to the hospital.' And I
don't want to go to the hospital. So I just
stay home.

"And my brother come to me and he
say, 'The reason you're sick is because
you're going to that Anglo meeting in
Santa Fe, and you're demonstrating.
You're just giving away our secrets and
then all those Anglos will take over
Navajo weaving. And nobody will want
Navajo rugs.' That's what he say.'' She
paused.

"Well, I didn't get no better. I keep saying 'I'm going to get better.' But I don't. So, pretty soon Sallie just say, 'I'm just going to take you, anyway.'

"And at the hospital they give me shots and feed me with a tube. And when they give me shots, I keep liquid down. But when they take the tube out, I throw up again. I lie in bed, and I put my head up, and the whole room goes around in circles. And if I try to stand up, I can't. And pretty soon I stay there two weeks, and I'm no better. I'm better with shots, and I'm no better when the shots stop. And the doctor tell me I need a ceremony. My body is O.K. But I don't get no better. And so my family take me home and we get a ceremony.

"After that, I still get dizzy. And another brother come to me. He talk to me, 'This is because you wrote that book, and you never should tell those Anglos about weaving.' After that my pick-up truck break down. And my other brother say, "You see, the witchcraft power was not strong enough to hurt you, but now it's got your truck.' That's what he say to me.

"And so I talk to my brother right then. I tell him, 'I write that book because I have a friend who ask me to write it. And I believe in what that book says. You say I'm giving the weaving to the Anglos. I'm not just giving it to them, I'm giving it to the *world*. And I give it to your grandchildren.

" 'Our Navajo girls don't weave no more. I have six daughters, and Noël is the only one who know weaving. And now there are other weavers out there. They are also my daughters, and I want them to know.

" 'You got a wife and she don't weave. You got daughters, and they don't weave. And after I'm dead, if their daughters want to weave, they'll learn from my book.'

"After that I get better."

T'áá áhót'é
T'áá áhót'é

T'áá áhót'é
T'áá áhót'é

I am White-Shell-Woman's child.
T'áá áhót'é
White-Shell-Woman is putting up the loom.
T'áá áhót'é
White-Shell-Woman is preparing now the loom.
T'áá áhót'é

I face the East.

Soft goods surround me.
T'áá áhót'é
Hard goods surround me.
T'áá áhót'é
Horses surround me.
T'áá áhót'é
Sheep surround me.
T'áá áhót'é
All buckskins continually coming
surround me.

There is beauty before me.

There is beauty behind me.

There is beauty above me.

There is beauty beneath me.

Beauty speaks from my mouth.
I am immortal.

    T'áá áhót'é   T'áá áhót'é   T'áá áhót'é   T'áá áhót'é

I Told The Audience Of Three Hundred

that Tiana Bighorse had agreed to come to Santa Fe to demonstrate at the 1980 Shared Horizons conference. I explained that she would be there throughout the three-day conference and her demonstrations would be open to them and to the general public. I wanted collectors to understand what goes into the rugs they own.

I explained she was a traditional weaver and had come from Tuba City. I hoped she would feel comfortable being there. And they could help.

If they did things in a Navajo way, she might feel more at home. I went on to tell them that on the reservation silences are lengthy, questions almost non-existent. When you want to know something, you watch. The Navajo learn visually.

However, I understood they were Anglo, and Anglos haven't been taught to learn that way. And I knew what I was asking would feel foreign. For that reason I would be specific.

"If you have a question you want to ask, put it in your simplest English. Next ask yourself, 'Is this what I really want to know?' If not, rethink and reword it. Then, after sitting a while in silence, ask the question quietly. If there's no response, don't ask again. Just wait.

"And even when the answer has come, don't say another word for at least three minutes. Look at your watch if you have to. Three minutes is a long time for an Anglo to keep quiet!

"I've learned that by waiting to ask a question, it's most often answered in the process. By asking a second question, immediately after the first, you miss the best of the answer, which is still to come."

The last day of the conference, after my breakfast session with Tiana, a newspaper lady asked if there was a time she and I could talk. She had missed my opening remarks and needed background information on the conference for her story. I told her we could meet at lunch.

"How is your story coming?" I asked sliding into the booth.

"Well, I just finished interviewing the Navajo weaver demonstrating here at the conference."

I winced at the use of the words

"interview" and "Navajo" in the same sentence. "Oh? How did it go?"

"Well," she said, "I don't think she understands English very well. I asked her some questions and she didn't answer right away and so I asked again. And still she didn't answer. She just kept weaving. Oh, she'd talk a little. And then she'd stop and so I'd just ask again."

I nodded, picturing the event.

"Well, after a time, we hadn't gotten very far. And so I thought maybe she didn't realize what an important newspaper I represent and how important my article is, and the conference, too. So I said to her, 'Now I want you to know that I represent a big newspaper and that there will be a lot of readers reading what I write and what you say. You tell all those readers what Navajo weaving means to you.'

"She still didn't understand what I was saying. She just looked down and kept weaving. And so I told her again: 'We want to hear what it feels like to have been weaving over fifty years. This is your opportunity to tell the world the significance of weaving for yourself and for your tribe and for people everywhere.'

"It was then she put her batten down and held her fork in her hand. I was almost ready to leave, thinking she didn't understand, when she finally looked at me and spoke. 'You write this,' she said. 'You tell all those people that when I sit here and weave, I'm just having fun.' "

Appendix

If you're interested in learning more about Navajo weaving techniques and philosophy, you can refer to my other books published by Northland Press.

But, if you who want to learn more about Navajo names—perhaps want one of your own—this is written for you. The ideas grew out of my storytelling, at workshops, among friends. And so I thank:

Passionate Coyote
The-One-Who-Makes-People-
    Understand
Golden Eagle
Rider
Channel
Old-Snorting-Buffalo
Water Strider
Seeking-Shadow-to-Wholeness
Calling Bird
Pine-Tree-Dancing-In-The-Wind
Bubbles
One-Who-Watches-Mountains
Sparkles-Across-The-Water
One-Who-Is-Considering-The-
    Question
SeesBeyond

One-Who-Talks-To-Trees
Barnacle
Self-Container
Earth-Tender
Prism
One-Who-Prefers-the-Shadow-
    and-the-Corner
One-Who-Rides-Side-Saddle
River-Running-To-The-Ocean
One-Who-Connects-In-word-
    and-Out-word
Pop! Goes the Weasel
Hawk, Soaring
Morning Star
Honer
Staccato Bird
Troll—on the Rainbow Bridge
Man-Who-Walks-The-Land
Running Woman
Mrs. Lefthand
Old-Man-Never-Sleeps
and the many others from whom I
    learned.

The Navajo, living as they do so closely with the elements, know them well. In a very real way the Sun, Wind, Rain and Snow belong to them. On reservation, when it is hot, you scorch; when the wind blows, you are sandblasted; when it rains, you get drenched; when it snows, you freeze. A hogan, devoid of central heating and air conditioning, does not insulate from the elements.

The Navajo phrase, "Díkwíísha nináahai" (How old are you?), is a telling one. Literally translated it becomes: "How many have you wintered?" As soon as a baby survives a winter, it is one.

Anglos admire native cultures for the extent to which they are in touch with nature, probably because the Anglo yearns for "something missing," without giving thought to how the out-of-touchness came to be. We go to great trouble to provide comfort and avoid discomfort. Temperature controlled, microwaved and T.V.ed homes bring the world into the living room, without our having to step forth into Earth, Fire, Water or Air. But the very act of insulating ourselves from the discomfort of the elements removes us from their meaning. Whereas living with them clarifies the internal resources we each call upon to "weather a storm" or "survive a winter."

A Navajo baby born at a Public Health Service Hospital is given a name for the hospital records in accordance with census regulations. That is, a family is not allowed to leave the hospital with "Baby Boy Begay." This "instant naming" is in direct contrast to Navajo tradition, wherein Grandfather carefully observes the baby for a year or two, and considers its most salient characteristic. Then he bestows a symbolic name.

Today, as a result of coexisting Anglo/Navajo naming practices, some Navajos have two names, one for census and one for self. The self-name sometimes stays constant for a lifetime and sometimes changes. Sometimes the census name is considered to be the only name. But the power of Navajo names and name-giving remains.

There was an old lady who had always been energetic, even in her nineties when I knew her. As she had never learned to drive, whenever she wanted to get from one distant hogan to another, or to the trading post, she would start off across the desert terrain at a veritable trot.

One hot afternoon Tiana Bighorse and I drove north of Tuba City to obtain a dye-plant called wild carrot.* The color-bearing roots grow two feet beneath the sandy surface, and extracting the dye-stuff requires much digging. As each root clump emerges, it is sorted: young tubers yield a valued orange dye, old ones a mustard color, "rotten" ones, a brown. Besides providing a wide range of hues, wild carrot, with its high tannic acid content, is one of the most colorfast of the native dyes. Throughout the tiring work, my friend and I discussed the excellence of this particular dye and our responsibility to its perpetuation. Before refilling each hole, we placed a young, moist tuber from each clump at the bottom: "Here's to the next year."

Since Tiana and I both needed an ample supply for the coming year, we dug all afternoon until the car was filled with tubers and heat stroke threatened. Back at her home, I split the roots in preparation for drying, and then divided and stashed our booty: mine in the jeep, hers under the bed.

Just as we sat down, through the hogan doorway I sighted a distant figure. Running toward us, it descended the mesa edge, briskly covering the long, hot stretch of flat sageland to the hogan, and soon I recognized the old lady. She made straight for the hogan, and immediately began sniffing her way around the space peering into every crevice, spouting a stream of Navajo words. "She says she smells wild carrots," Tiana looked at me knowingly. Around the hogan her friend darted, checking behind the wood-burning stove, under bags of wool, and surely, ever so surely, edging toward the bed. Moments later, down on hands and knees, she pulled out the dye stuffs we had just stashed. In no time at all, according to Navajo protocol, Tiana had divided up her cache of carrots to share with her clan relative.

The one who effortlessly covered the reservation at a dead trot, whose internal engine was always revved, even in her nineties, this one was called "Running-Woman."

---

*Rumex hymenosepalis (Bot.); Canyaigre, sorrel (Eng.); Chaat'ínii (Nav.).

For one medicineman in Tuba City, the tradition of continuous ceremonial chanting in all-night ceremonies was an Absolute; an interrupted song could undo the entire ritual. Younger apprentices, with less dedication to the medicine way, argued that the responsiblity lay with the *group* of Singers; as long as one voice carried the chant, the song could be considered whole.

But this old man persisted in his more strenuous path, steadfastly resisting the temptation to snooze while others sang. His unyielding personal integrity is implied in his name:

"Old-Man-Never-Sleeps."

While teaching a series of weaving workshops at the Denver Museum of Natural History, I met David Baysinger, an audiovisual expert with the museum and Rita Lovato, a TV reporter of city cultural events. I talked with them about Navajo names. Later, the two filmed a museum documentary on Navajo sandpainter, Baatsoɬání. The final edited segment explores the subject of the Navajo name; appropriately, it retains many of the long natural Navajo silences.

In one scene, Rita's voice makes a piquant counterpoint to the sandpainter's silent, complex rendering on the hogan floor.

"On the bottom of the commercial sandpaintings you sell, you put the name Baatsoɬání'. Can you tell me what this means?"

Silence. Unhurried, traditional placement of tiny colored sand-lines.

"It's a name my Grandfather gave me when I was young."

The camera remains steady. No flicker of sound or scene change fills the gap— only sand flowing surely from a tiny hole between three attenuated fingers.

"I was about two when my grandfather gave me that name."

Rita's position and expression remain unchanged, an expectant waiting charges the moment. "It means, 'The-One-Who-Collects-Many-Feathers.' "

"Do you still collect feathers?"

A single unit of the design being constructed grain by grain fills the screen as it does the concentration of the maker.

"Oh, yes."

"How many feathers do you have?"

At this question, Baatsolání shifts his body as though his work is complete. The camera pans back to catch his face scanning the image. He laughs knowingly.

"Not enough!"

The camera, still panning backwards, reveals for the first time the whole sandpainting. It fills the floor of the hogan. Radiating from the center outward to each wall is a rainbow of earthy, muted ceremonial feathers.

Soon after I became aware of Navajo names, I noticed that people seldom spoke them. I was researching the antique process of urine-fermented indigo and a weaver had told me I needed a large Navajo pitch pot. Trading posts didn't have any big enough, so I asked a traditional potter from Shonto to make one for me.

When it was done, the potter brought it to me accompanied by her English-speaking thirty-year-old son. Between my limited Navajo and her son's translations, we first talked of weaving—later about the pot.

I didn't have cash on hand, so I wrote a check for twenty-five dollars. But the phrases I had learned in Navajo language class didn't include "What is your name?" I switched to English, looked in the direction of the son, and inquired obliquely,

"What name shall I write on the check?"

The son said something to his mother in Navajo and left the room. In silence I sat with Potter-Who-Speaks-No-English.

Why hadn't her son answered? Why did he leave? I knew enough not to ask again, so I simply waited.

After a while the potter rose and shuffled slowly across the room. She withdrew a small piece of paper from her purse and silently set it on my partially filled-out check.

It was her social security card.

Many months later, as I sat spinning with Tiana Bighorse, I told her the story of the pitch pot. I had never fully understood what had happened.

"It's bad luck to say your own name," Tiana explained. "It's not quite so bad if somebody else say it when you stand right there. Not too bad if somebody say it after you go."

I continued to spin the silence, making space for whatever might be coming.

"You just have to save your name for when you're in a tight spot."

I urgently wondered what a "tight spot" meant, but I kept my eyes on the revolving whorl and the yarn that was thinning. Several rolags later she clarified.

"In the old days, in my father's day, a tight spot is being in a box canyon. And the calvary is coming."

The image of that box canyon has stayed with me and gained in significance through the years. Just before my son Shawn went into the Navy, I discussed with him Navajo names, his in particular. In the flippant way of a twenty-year-old, he remarked:

"I can understand that. If your name is 'Running Deer'—you'd better start running. And if your name is 'Slinging Bull'—you'd better start talking."

Yes. In a tight spot, if your name truly reflects you and your resources, calling on

it tells you how to get out.

There is something compelling about the box canyon, about saying or not saying a name aloud, about the name itself. It revolves in the mind, collects greater meaning, generates questions:

What is a box canyon?
In Tiana's father's time, a box canyon was a place to go for protection. But it might turn out to be a trap.

Are there contemporary equivalents of a box canyon?
Marriage?
Job security?
Being a mother?
Retirement?
Probably more. Depending on our reasons for entering into these terrain pockets and how we handle them, all can be dead ends. Traps.

What is the effect of saying a name aloud?
Perhaps it helps to look to the structure and oral tradition of the Navajo language.

In Navajo, a noun or name often encompasses an object's core quality: what it is and does, how it functions in its environment, sometimes even how it looks. For instance, the word "Tsé'ésdazii," Mountain Mahogany,* translates literally as "that which is heavy as rock." Here the name cites weight and density as primary qualities. A weaver would know to use it for a heavy, abrasion-resistant weaving fork.

To the Navajo, word and object are nearly indistinguishable. For instance, the word "Shash" (bear) is never said aloud in the winter when bears are asleep; pronouncing it would call them out from hibernation and bring bad luck. So, in this orally traditioned culture, the specific act of *saying* a word can connect directly with the spirit of the object.

What's in a name?
Navajo word distinctions among observed things are very precise. Seven different words describe distinct kinds of lightning; there is no generic form for lightning. By the distinctness of each word, each kind of lightning is simultaneously described and differentiated from any other kind.

A child playing at home—growing, being—is similarly named.

---

*Cercocarpis Montanus (Bot.).

Birthing A Name

Most of us don't have Grandfather standing about, watching and contemplating the gifting of our name. In truth, we are no longer two years old. Nor are we Navajo. And though some of us would rather be gifted with a name instead of going through the labor of birthing it ourselves, ultimately the responsibility and knowledge lie within. This section is written for anyone who would like a name to call on in future box canyons.

The first step in the naming process is to release the conscience to be "humble"—to stop denying our outstanding qualities as though they lessen those of others. Clearly, what we are does not diminish what anyone else is. Each of us is unique and perfect and whole in a different way. And we are out to name that uniqueness.

To help identify your specialness, look for constancy—the quality that has been since birth, and that will be for life. For though we change homes, jobs, skills, marriages, etc., there is a part of us that remains constant and we bring it to each situation. It is an energy source, an essential essence—an unchanging core.

To approach your core, start with these two questions:

What quality gets me the furthest?
What quality gets me into the most trouble?

List the qualities that come to mind without judgement. Keep the flow open and write them down as they come, without regard to whether they are "good," "bad," "desirable," "undesirable." Devoid of judgement, qualities of the core simply "are." Remember, you are not naming what you wish you were; nor are you naming what you fear you are. You are naming what is.

As you begin trying on words, an important realization may come: When you are speaking the deepest truth, the answers to both questions are exactly the same.

The duality of a characteristic is clearest in someone we are close to—a spouse, parent, child. The same quality we are most attracted to sometimes becomes overbearing. For instance, if we married for security, there are times our spouse seems too secure—even boring, rigid. If we were attracted by an exciting visionary kind of person, that person may sometimes seem unpredictable, scattered. The very quality in another that is most difficult for us to relate to is simply the flip side of the one we enjoy most.

So we can't ask people to change—to be other than what they are. To change would be the death of their core—their source of life-energy. It is the same with ourselves.

With these ideas in mind, restructure the questions:

Which of my qualities is most appealing to others?
Which is most difficult to get along with?

Perhaps you've noticed. All four questions are identical. So the answers are identical. Take time now and enjoy the process. Don't get impatient and try to rush it. Don't procrastinate and let it go because it's illusive or because you're not used to thinking in these terms.

Consider the questions when you're relaxed—when you first awaken in the morning, while in a warm tub, while driving on a long trip. In places of suspended time.

When the list feels complete, distill it. Some words overlap. Some words are manifestations of something more pervasive, deeper. Simplify, clarify, sort and re-sort until the resulting descriptive words "feel right." Then give them form:

The one who_____ ;
The weaver who_____ ;
The woman who_____ ;
The man who_____ .

The descriptive phrase is just a start. Ahead lies the symbolic name that touches the spirit.

The Symbolic Name

In my weaving workshops, I told and retold the Navajo stories. With time, I came to understand them in a greater depth; I was experiencing the power of the Navajo oral tradition. The very act of saying words out loud gives a story tangibility and accessibility. At times the "chance" juxtaposition of two different stories lends insight. Other times a coincidental choice of words brings new understanding. And through these workshops I came to know the importance of the symbolic name-form.

On the first day of one workshop, I noticed a particular student with a weaverly, earthy sort of appearance. She wore a denim skirt, a hand-woven sash belt, an ethnic blouse. Her name was Gail.

The next day when the class reconvened, in the midst of the newly familiar faces, I spotted a total stranger. Her low cut dress and hair scooped up on top of her head lent a sexy, carefree look. I thought she was a new student joining the class a day late. After the morning's orientation, students returned to their Navajo looms for hands-on weaving work. But instead of coming up to talk with me, the unidentified one went to the loom at which Gail had woven the day before. Could that be Gail?

The third morning there was another

stranger among us. This one had braided pigtails and wore oversized, floppy Oshkosh jeans. She looked like she was just off the farm. Again after orientation the stranger went to Gail's loom. I now held three very different images for one name, "Gail."

Later in the day, Gail and I conferred about the design she was weaving. She was at the center of her pattern where remarkable things happen. She had a willful, irreverent way of changing her design, wildly and freely transforming entire passages, unmindful that such radical changes would require massive raveling and reweaving. Later, when the class began evolving "Navajo" names for themselves, I suggested to Gail the word "willful."

"Willful, that's me!" she exclaimed, trying the word on for sound. Someone else said to her laughingly, "Yeah, and you're a little perverse, too!" While I cringed, thinking of the word's negative connotation, Gail embraced it triumphantly, "That's what I am— 'The-One-With-Perverse-Willfulness!' " She said it with conviction.

During the following days, as others refined their descriptive names, Gail kept hers. She said it felt right. The final day, I asked the group to change their approach: switch off the intellectual; permit the symbolic intuitive to range freely; find their metaphorical name. A friend turned to Gail.

"Can I tell you about the day I first met you?" Gail nodded.

"I remember the first day I ever saw you. You came to my house on a horse. You were riding a western saddle and you had on a dress. The thing that has always stuck in my mind about that moment is you were riding side-saddle."

Gail's name crystalized instantly. True to core, irreverent of convention, Gail became "The-One-Who-Rides-Side-Saddle."

There is a leap that occurs from the descriptive to the symbolic. While the descriptive name is quite literal, the symbolic name approximates the spirit. "The-One-Who-Rides-Side-Saddle" calls forth an oblique, moving, willful entity never quite lined up with what others expect.

And that which aptly names a part, names the whole. The ever-present core indelibly marks each action—riding a horse, dressing for a workshop, designing a rug. It can do no other.

To lift your name from the descriptive to the symbolic, work intuitively. Keep your intent in the forefront of your mind. Expect the name to come. Proceed with the course of living; your name is on its way.

At its arrival, celebrate! Create a ritual in welcome. Take time to get acquainted; this is the begining of an important relationship.

Calling On Your Name
In Box Canyons

In one of my Oregon classes a young woman sought a name to express both her visionary abilities and how she sometimes neglected the present when dealing with the beyond.

When she returned home after the workshop, she experienced a repetition of an old wound: the cornea of her eye spontaneously tore. When it continued to tear, she sought medical help. Doctors recommended surgery; she personally felt there must be an alternative solution even though the physicians offered none. In the coldness of her home, she sat with eyes closed and covered, enshrouded in blackness, her confusion compounded by pain.

The day before her surgery, she grew desperate. She knew her present condition had to do with her body's inability to heal. If it couldn't heal itself now, how would it handle surgery? When she posed these questions to her physicians, they only became irate. Suddenly, she realized she was in a "box canyon" of a very real sort. She thought to call on her newly taken name, to focus on her core quality, to search beyond the present for the answer.

She decided her doctors might be good technicians, but they were not healers. She would have to find a way and cure herself. She phoned old friends who were teaching macrobiotics at an institute in Boston. They concurred with her insight and urged her to nourish herself, recommending dietary changes and external eye treatments. After a month of following this routine, her eye had fully healed. The doctors were amazed. Perhaps they had underestimated the resources of "Seesbeyond."

Calling On Your Name:
To Empower The Creative Process

The composition depicts an adobe worker in the moment of scooping mud to apply to a wall. But the artist wants to elevate this mundane moment, to transcend the ordinary, address a Universal. But how?

Artist's journal entry:

> I am crouched on the floor of the studio, legs and feet tucked beneath, wrists crossed behind my back. I am examining in minute detail the content of my current work, head moving back and forth, scanning, scanning, focusing directly ahead, all external stimuli excluded from my senses.
>
> Perspective is needed and I prepare for flight. With a symbolic ruffling of feathers and a shrill cry of purpose, I launch. Powerful wings extended, soaring, circling, feather-tips sensing the gentle thermals, I gain precious altitude. From this lofty sky eyrie the entire landscape opens. With raptor vision, I can scan the total scene and also pin-point the smallest object. I focus on the tiny image of the adobe worker far below, merging him and his universe.
>
> There's the gesture, the scooping of adobe. But at that instant, in mid-motion, the worker hesitates. In the living mud-mass before him, he has seen his reflection! Unity of wall, mud and man.
>
> The relationship is clear; the hunt has yielded. Talons poised, I plummet and connect.

Working with the core can empower the creative process. You can create from your core to infuse your work with your own uniqueness. And you can approach the subject of your work—name its core and clarify the content.

But in the end, when you're in the

right place, core of artist and core of content will be the same.

Calling On Your Name: To Relate Intimately To Another

A man, with vision farther than most mortals care to reach. Propensity to lose himself in ideas and abstractions. Flights of the imagination. Dogged conceptual pursuit. These qualities suggest the name, "Eagle."

A skilled horsewoman. A thrill of harnessing energies larger than the self. An eye for detail. A skilled trainer. A tendency to "nag." Perhaps the name, "Rider."

Rider's attraction to Eagle is in the thrill of harnessing large forces. In return, as a sensitive equestrian, she offers him a wise, gentle guidance and facility in handling the multitude of attendant details. Their connection, of rider to ridden, assures them of intimacy and close contact.

But, the same qualities that bind them can emerge in conflict. Often rider must ask herself if her wisdom is adequate to the task. When should she tighten the rein? When give Eagle his lead? Is the time and energy required to domesticate the wild, worth it?

How high could I fly? How far could I soar without Rider, Eagle asks when he feels deadweight. For, despite training in falconry to serve man, eagles often return to the wild.

As with any relationship, Eagle and Rider will constantly need to muster energy and creativity to nourish themselves, their mates, the relationship. And there will be excitement in the struggle as well as in the union.

If you would like to explore your name in concert with another, start by identifying the strengths of each person. Then, brainstorm how you can capitalize on this combination of qualities. Next, identify the difficulties of these strengths coming together.

You can explore these areas with a relaxed attitude—even a joyful humor—when you remember that neither person is to blame for difficulties. The conflict you are exploring is the simple result of core qualities coming together. When you know the core to be the source of energy and life, you have no wish to change yourself or the other. To do so would dissolve the Self—or the relationship.

And, if you do dissolve the relationship and form a new one, don't be surprised when variations of the same conflict reappear. The core comes with you. The challenge is in working with it and making it a source of energy that furthers you and others.

Calling on Your Name:
At The Mid-Way Point

Many a weaver working on a finite warp* has asked:

> Do I have the ability to bring into
> being what I see in my mind?
> Will the design in my mind fit the
> physical warp?
> Will my colors contrast enough to
> carry from a distance?
> Will they contrast too much?
> Have I dyed enough wool of each
> color?

Life, like the Navajo warp, is also finite, with a precise beginning and end. So perhaps its questions are parallel:

> Do I have the ability to actualize what
> I have envisioned?
> Can I fit what I want to do within my
> finite lifespan?
> Will what I am doing be noticed by
> others (carry from a distance)?
> Will I stand out too much?
> Will my personal resources endure to
> the end?

Navajo rug designs are bilaterally symmetrical—the top half mirrors the bottom half. So the weaver must constantly measure where she is in relation to the half. In order to weave what her mind has envisioned, at the mid-way point she must have completed half the design. But there are many variables in weaving—the packing may be heavy or

---

*The Navajo weaver warps her loom for each rug separately. This establishes irrevocable parameters—precise bottom and top. And she must fit her design between the two. Looms of many other cultures are warped for multiple rugs, so beginning and ending points are imprecise.

light, the warp spaces large or small, the weft yarn thin or thick. There are many reasons why the center of the envisioned design often falls short of the center of the warp. When this happens, more design must be created to fill the space.

But just as frequently, the envisioned half turns out to be larger than its physically alotted space. Then, the design must be cut back and the weaver's expectations reduced.

Perhaps approaching the mid-way point on the rug is like approaching mid-life. Both require reevaluation. At the half, our irrevocable first-half decisions may seem limiting—the idea of changing how we thought things were going to be, disorienting, frightening.

But unlike our single opportunity with life, in weaving there are many rugs. So in weaving, we encounter the half repeatedly and through this process learn skills for its navigation. In time, the center seems not a place of anxiety, but one of anticipation, excitement, growth.

One key is knowing from the start that when we get to the half we will be making changes for the better. For, the nearer we get to the half, the more we know and the better will be our decisions. Now we can clearly see warp spacing, packing, remaining quantities of wool colors. We also know our own personal abilities, limitations and pacing. So, design solutions at the half are always better than those envisioned at the beginning!

With repeated weavings, we also find that once the decision has been made and a new direction determined, the actual task of ripping out and reweaving is actually a pleasant one. The test lies in letting go of the old and knowing that a better, more viable solution exists. It does.

And if at the half we need help clarifying alternatives and evoking the right solution, we can always call on our name.

Calling on Your Name: In The End

We can only create out of our core, so everything we do reflects who we are. Our home. Our lifestyle. Our finished rug on the loom. If we want insight into who we are, we can read our own rug design.

Here are some questions we might ask:

How is this design like me or like my life right now?

Does the main design dominate or blend with the background? (Do I dominate or flow with my environment?)

How much touching or separateness have I given to the designs?

How much space does each object require? (How much touching, separateness, space do I like for myself?)

How does the design relate to the edge of the textile? (Do I test boundaries or stay back from them?)

As we continue to resolve the second half of our weaving, life analogies continue. Patterns reverse out, decrease and terminate. The weaver feels a sense of joyful relief as each early commitment is fulfilled and released.

The remaining warp space becomes smaller and tighter, the progress slower. The rug that once showed progress minute by minute now requires an eternity row by row. We know from experience that the final inches require infinite patience. To do them well, we must bring to them the same kind of energy we brought to the rest of the piece. Here it helps to keep in mind the final line of the Navajo Beauty Way chant:

In Beauty, it is finished.

There is no way to hurry the pace. The body starts to slow, heart beat, breathing. But, we can disempower time. We can slow down and get in touch with the process. We can tap our energy source. Bring beauty to the end. This is the way to finish a rug.

Each well-navigated weaving ends in this way. Each well-navigated ending prepares us for others: the end of a project; the end of a relationship; the end of a life.

"You Can Always Tell a Medicineman . . ."

Jack had come home from the hospital later than usual. From the kitchen where I was preparing dinner, I watched him sink into the chair across the room. His face was white.

"I don't want to talk right now."

It was much later when he told me. He was on his way home from the hospital when he heard a Navajo nurse call to him from one of the rooms. He found her standing by an old medicineman. "You can always tell a medicineman," he told me. "There is something about their personal power that is unmistakable."

The nurse explained in English that the old man was on dialysis and wished to be disconnected. She had protested he would die; he replied he knew that and repeated his wish. The nurse had insisted she didn't have the authority to disconnect him; only a doctor could make that decision; she would do it only under orders. He told her to find one. "And just then you walked by, Dr. Bennett."

Now the patient looked directly at Jack and began to tell his story. The nurse interpreted.

I can tell you are powerful in medicine. One always recognizes it in another. For my whole life I have followed the medicine-path. When I was young I learned the simple healing ceremonies. When I got older I learned the harder ones. Some it took me years to learn. I know some few men know. I traveled far across the reservation and beyond. And wherever I went, people knew my power and asked me to heal them. For this I earned the name, "The-Man-Who-Walks-The-Land." And by this name I am honored.

I want to tell you something. The more powerful you are, the more important it is to know the line of good and bad. And the harder it is to walk that line. I can say now, I never crossed over. I always used my power for good. Of this I am proud.

I say to you now, disconnect me from this machine. If I stay on it and return to my people, my name will become, "The-Man-Who-Must-Pee-Through-A-Tube." I would rather die.

Jack had only recently taken the Hippocratic Oath. "I just stood there thinking about what he said. Thinking about what he said. And pretty soon I decided that there was only one right thing to do. 'It's your choice,' I told him. And I knew that having made the decision, I couldn't tell the nurse to do it; I had to do it myself. So I just reached down and disconnected him from the machine."

Now, more than fifteen years later, the story of The-Man-Who-Walks-The-Land is still with me.

Why?

First, it deals with our right to our own death.

Second, it has occurred to me that the medicineman called on his name to get himself out of what is perhaps the final "box canyon."

And third, it worked.